Penguin Modern Poets
VOLUME 6

U. A. Fanthorpe was born in Kent in 1929 and educated at St Anne's College, Oxford. She began work conventionally by teaching at Cheltenham, but then became a Hoover's telephone clerk, a hospital receptionist, a writer-in-residence and other more questionable things. She has published six poetry collections, the latest being *Neck-Verse* (1992) and *Safe as Houses* (1995), and has won some awards. In 1994 she was the first woman to be nominated for the role of Oxford Professor of Poetry. She gravitated to Gloucestershire at an early age and has lived there ever since.

Elma Mitchell was born at Airdrie, Scotland, in 1919. She is a professional librarian and has worked in broadcasting, publishing and journalism in London, but is now living in Somerset, where she works as a freelance writer and translator. She is the author of four collections of poetry, all published by Peterloo Poets: *The Poor Man in the Flesh* (1976), *The Human Cage* (1979), *Furnished Rooms* (1983) and *People Etcetera: Poems New & Selected* (1987). Her first collection was a runner-up in The Arts Council of Great Britain and Provincial Booksellers' Fairs Association Poetry Award for 1977. In the same year she was one of the five first-prize winners in the Cheltenham Festival of Literature Poetry Competition.

Charles Causley was born in Launceston, Cornwall, in 1917. After serving for six years in the Royal Navy during World War II he taught for many years in his native town before becoming a full-time writer. His first book of poems, *Farewell, Aggie Weston*, appeared in 1951 and since then he has published many collections both for adults and children. He is a Fellow of the Royal Society of Literature and in 1967 was awarded the Queen's Gold Medal for Poetry. He has also received a number of literary prizes, including a Cholmondeley Award in 1971, the Kurt Maschler Award in 1987 and the Ingersoll/ T.S. Eliot Award in 1990. In 1986 Charles Causley was appointed CBE. His updated *Collected Poems* appeared in 1992.

The Penguin Modern Poets Series

Volume One
James Fenton
Blake Morrison
Kit Wright

Volume Two
Carol Ann Duffy
Vicki Feaver
Eavan Boland

Volume Three
Glyn Maxwell
Mick Imlah
Peter Reading

Volume Four
Liz Lochhead
Roger McGough
Sharon Olds

Volume Five
Simon Armitage
Sean O'Brien
Tony Harrison

Volume Six
U. A. Fanthorpe
Elma Mitchell
Charles Causley

Penguin Modern Poets

VOLUME 6

U. A. FANTHORPE

ELMA MITCHELL

CHARLES CAUSLEY

PENGUIN BOOKS

Published by the Penguin Group
Penguin Books Ltd, 27 Wrights Lane, London w8 5TZ, England
Penguin Books USA Inc., 375 Hudson Street, New York, New York 10014, USA
Penguin Books Australia Ltd, Ringwood, Victoria, Australia
Penguin Books Canada Ltd, 10 Alcorn Avenue, Toronto, Ontario, Canada M4V 3B2
Penguin Books (NZ) Ltd, 182–190 Wairau Road, Auckland 10, New Zealand

Penguin Books Ltd, Registered Offices: Harmondsworth, Middlesex, England

This selection first published 1996
10 9 8 7 6 5 4 3 2 1

Filmset by Datix International Limited, Bungay, Suffolk
Printed in England by Clays Ltd, St Ives plc
Set in Monophoto Garamond

Contents

U. A. Fanthorpe

Poem for Oscar Wilde	3
Job Description: Medical Records	4
Resuscitation Team	6
Tyneside in December	7
Second Time Round	8
Cluny: Five Senses, Two Beasts and a Lady	9
Deer in Gowbarrow Park	12
At Cowan Bridge	14
Dear Mr Lee	16
'Very quiet here'	18
At Averham	19
A Wartime Education	21
Washing-up	23
7301	25
Old Man, Old Man	26
Looking for Jorvik	28
Homing In	30
Teacher's Christmas	31
Unfinished Chronicle	32
The Comforters	35
Costa Geriatrica	37
Superannuated Psychiatrist	39
Reception in Bristol	40
Titania to Bottom	41
Neck-Verse	42
Awkward Subject	44
The Room Where Everyone Goes	45
Counting Song	47
A Major Road for Romney Marsh	49
Odysseus' Cat	50

On Worms, and Being Lucky 52
What, in Our House? 54
DNA 56
Collateral Damage 57

Elma Mitchell

Thoughts after Ruskin 61
The Corset 63
Alice Uglier 64
Hanging Out the Wash 66
Winter in Lodgings 67
Late Fall 69
The Last of the Rain 70
Turning Out the Mattresses 72
At First, My Daughter 73
Mother, Dear Mother 74
Vulnerable 75
Cook Speaks 76
Recreation 77
Propitiation 78
How Was It Up There? 79
Wonderful 80
Life-cycle of the Moth 81
Monorhyme 82
It's the Sea I Want 83
From the Somerset Levels 86
Directions for Taking 88
This Poem . . . 89
People Etcetera 90
The Death of Adam 92
The Watch-Dogs 94
The Passenger Opposite 95
Water Aubrey 97
Country Life 98

from Furnished Rooms

    Notice   99
    Sculptress   100
    It's Mother, You See   101
    Letter Home   102
    Self-Portraits   103
    Expatriate   104
    Room Mates   104
    Last Words   105
    All Out   105

Charles Causley

    Kelly Wood   109
    Family Feeling   110
    Bridie Wiles   111
    Dick Lander   113
    First Day   115
    My Enemy   116
    Forbidden Games   118
    The Boot Man   119
    Recruiting Drive   120
    Chief Petty Officer   122
    Richard Bartlett   124
    Uncle Stan   126
    Photograph   128
    I Love the Laurel Green   129
    Ballad of the Bread Man   130
    At the British War Cemetery, Bayeux   133
    I am the Great Sun   134
    Night before a Journey   135
    Flying   136
    Grandmother   138
    Friedrich   140
    At the Church of St Anthony, Lisbon   142

Ten Types of Hospital Visitor   144
At St Hilary   150
Eden Rock   151

Acknowledgements   152

U.A. Fanthorpe

Poem for Oscar Wilde

Lane is cutting cucumber
Sandwiches, and the dogcart
Is coming round at the same
Time next week. The weather
Continues charming.

Reading Gaol and seedy France
Lurk in Cecily's garden
Under the pink roses. As
A man sows, so let him reap.
This truth is rarely pure,
And never simple.

Babies, handbags and lives are
Abandoned (I use the word
In the sense of *lost* or *mislaid*).
Sin, a temperance beverage,
Has stained somebody's lining.

This exquisite egg, which hatched
Ruin for you, who made it,
Retains its delicate poise.
Grief turns hair gold, and teacake
Can be tragic. The weather
Continues charming.

Job Description: Medical Records

Innocence is important, and order.
You need have no truck with the
Seamy insides of notes, where blood
And malignant growths and indelicate

Photographs wait to alarm. We like
To preserve innocence. You will
Be safe here, under the permanent
Striplighting. (Twenty-four hours cover.

Someone is always here. Our notes
Require constant company.) No
Patients, of course. The porter comes
And goes, but doesn't belong. With

His hairless satyr's grin, he knows
More than is suitable. Your conversation
Should concern football and television.
You may laugh at his dirty jokes,

But not tell any. Operations
Are not discussed here. How, by
The way, is your imagination?
Poorly, I hope. We do not encourage

Speculation in clerks. We prefer you
To think of patients not as people, but
Digits. That makes it much easier. Our system
Is terminal digit filing. If you

Are the right type for us, you will be
Unconscious of overtones. The contrasting
Weights of histories (puffy
For the truly ill, thin and clean

For childhood's greenstick fractures)
Will not concern you. You will use
The Death Book as a matter of routine.
Our shelves are tall, our files heavy. Have you

A strong back and a good head for heights?

Resuscitation Team

Arrives like a jinn, instantly,
Equipped with beards, white coats, its own smell,
And armfuls of metal and rubber.

Deploys promptly round the quiet bed
With horseplay and howls of laughter.
We, who are used to life, are surprised

At this larky resurrection. Runs
Through its box of tricks, prick, poke and biff,
While we watch, amazed. The indifferent patient

Is not amused, but carries little weight,
Being stripped and fumbled
By so many rugger-players. My first corpse,

If she is a corpse, lies there showing
Too much breast and leg. The team
Rowdily throws up the sponge, demands soap and water,

Leaves at the double. One of us,
Uncertainly, rearranges the night-dress.
Is it professional to observe the proprieties

Now of her who leaves privately
Wheeled past closed doors, her face
Still in the rictus of victory?

Tyneside in December

For Bill Bailey

Here wind and darkness rule;
Have rubbed out the intention
Of landscape, the intrusion of trees.

The race has adjusted, has grown
Four-square double-glazed houses
For four-square practical people,
And small square gardens for long-
rooted indestructible rose-trees.

Here households practise existence by vivid
Electric embers, hymning home-baked
Hospitality and putting on weight.
Here law-fearing straight streets
Glow orange and violet by night
For ten o'clock's dauntless dog-walkers.

And the lighthouse is saying something
Comprehensible only to men at sea.

By a shivering tallow dip, here
In the old, unimaginable darkness and wind,
Bede soberly sifted miraculous evidence,
Divined the shape of the unmapped
Country's history, keeping the candle
From going out. And out
There, in the darkness, the wind and the rain,
Cuthbert practised the habit of being holy.

Second Time Round

Is it the past or the future they endorse?

The past, where both chose someone
Other, since discreetly departed,
Leaving mementoes like testy elderly terriers,
A stray grandchild or so,
And a nice little nest-egg, snugly invested?

Or the future, delicately indented
By his false-toothy smile and hearing aid,
Her look of mutton, expensively dressed
To look like mutton? How many years
Before the discreet departed get them down?

We know why wedding guests attend:
They come for the jamboree, to keep in touch,
From curiosity, perhaps, or perhaps
Because Mum brought them.

But the happy couple, so garlanded,
So old, with their safe deposits
And shaky health, their taut smiles aimed
Down the short barren aisle of the future –
Do they redress some colossal
Incarnate error, the second time round?

No. These lovers are victims
Of Hymen's awful idol,
That poses so sullenly, legged,
Tiered and anointed with ice,
By the bride and the groom and the knife
On the album's last page.

Cluny: Five Senses, Two Beasts and a Lady

For Lindis Masterman

Unicorn eyes his head
In the lady's mirror. His tail has turned
Perpendicular with excitement as her hand lies
Human on his withers. Two cloven feet
Rest on her lap. This is for Lindis,
Who led me among the astute French faces,
Highbrow graffiti, imperial strut of trees,
Corks in the well-rinsed gutters, painted
Pools of Giverny. Lion looks out
Of his century at us. You can see his tongue.
He is trying not to snigger. *La Voie*.

With eight fingers and two thumbs the lady
Handles her portable organ. Her maid
Works the bellows gingerly,
Without conviction. Unicorn, who
Adores music, is capering mediaevally.
Language of elegant intercourse: *pardon, madame;*
Madame, je vous en prie. Merci, Lindis,
For the old man in the train admiring your accent,
Who gave us flowers, the girl dancing to
'Tea for Two' at night in a street café.
L'Ouïe. Lion's expression is equivocal.

Monkey has a sugarplum, so has Parrot.
Lapdog is willing the lady
To remember him too. Unicorn,
Having counted the calories,
Turns his head away. You can see
His double chin. Ah Lindis, the bread

And the ices and fruit, the impromptu
Memorable meals! The taste of lettuce!
Lion is frankly greedy. His toothy jaws
Are wide open. He might even
Be roaring. *Le Goût*.

Monkey, in a *jacquerie* haircut,
Snuffs a carnation. The lady
Creates something clever with flowers
And florist's wire. Her maid looks critical
(She has done the advanced course).
Inhaling the aromatic shopgirls
With Lindis, the aseptic Métro,
Probing noses bedded in Monet's chubby peonies.
Unicorn beams. He enjoys this
Petit Trianon lifestyle. *L'Odorat*.
Lion is trying to look naïve.

Unicorn is having his horn stroked
By the lady. He is thrilled to bits;
His ears are askew with
Respectful passion. Lindis explains
The art of making salad. Insular hands
Explore the sober shapely planes
Of everyday ware. Glancing encounters
With foreign skin, with paving stones that cry *Mort
Héroïquement pour la France*. Lion's face bulges
With suppressed giggles. He is trying
To catch our eye. *Le Toucher*.

The lady discards her jewels;
This signifies free will. Her maid
Is looking poised. Lion and Unicorn
Have reverted to heraldry, null
As supporters on a By Appointment shopfront.

The teacher rubs in the moral: *Vous pouvez devenir*
Esclaves de vos passions de bonbons.
Her manycoloured infants digest the formula.
They are learning the art of
Being French. *A mon seul désir*
Says the tent, unexpectedly.

Lindis has led me through the tapestry
Into France, among flowering
Sonorous abstractions, martial trees;
Into a promised home county, where Rabbit,
Fox, Lamb, Wolf, Goat, Panther and Duck
Amble among the mille-fleur marginalia,
While Danton and St Louis, masquerading
As Tenniel's familiars, frisk
For Marie-Antoinette, who is also Alice,
And they all speak a language
Which I cannot pronounce, but I know.

Deer in Gowbarrow Park

For David Webb

Not a gallant old warhorse of a poem,
Scarred from the student wars, but an indomitable
Little hackney, docile with twelve-year-olds,
Who may not understand *inner eyes* and
Tranquil recollecting, but know a *King Alfred*
When they see one, and can imagine lots.

Years later William knocked it together;
Mary gave her two lines. But it was Dorothy
Did the fieldwork, across the daffodilled years,
On a threatening misty morning, April,
1802. A boat is floating in the middle
Of the bay. Cows cause a diversion.
They see that yellow flower that Mrs C.
Calls *pilewort*; wood-sorrell; daffodils, naturally,

Waves at different distances, and rain,
And a sour landlady (*it is her way*),
And excellent ham and potatoes. Warm rum
And water for two – seven shillings all told.
We enjoyed ourselves, she says, *and wished
For Mary*. You hand us that day,

Dorothy, sister, all the random details, the furze bush
Opposite Mr Clarkson's, dry clothes afterwards,
William reading Congreve by the fire, how it rained
When you went to bed, and *N.B. Deer
In Gowbarrow Park like skeletons*,
With, of course, daffodils, *about the breadth
Of a country turnpike road*.

From William and Mary the official version,
Framed, in focus, ready to be declaimed,
Public as tapestry, concluding with a Thought.
The National Trust can use a poem like this.
But your straggle of unplanned delights and scrambles,
Texture of wind and wetness, glancing
Touch of the day, like (N.B.) the Gowbarrow deer
Defy the taming mind, your presence just
An urgent breathless charge: *N.B.*, *N.B.*

The woman here is Dorothy, whose journal entry for 15 April
1802 was used by William to write the poem 'Daffodils' in 1804.
Mary gave her two lines: Mary's lines are:

    They flash upon that inward eye
    Which is the bliss of solitude

At Cowan Bridge

For Elsa Corbluth

This place has elected to lie low.
Houses are called *Private Road*
And *Private Property*.

Everything is ostentatiously eating:
Free-ranging hens and geese, a fat horse,
A goat tethered to its larder.
Black-snouted lambs nuzzle and crop.
The local store sells local lemon curd.
Two miles away at the teashop they hope
To delight your palate, and restore
Those jaded tastebuds.

And dandelions do well. Their mop heads stare
Up at the sun. But the scrawny ash
Hugs back its green.

Discreet of you not to die here,
Maria, Elizabeth, elder daughters,
Who caught death here.
The river's a true witness. It sings
A bleak song: children were cold here,
And children were hungry. The lion-headed fell
Averts its gaze, but you can see where winter
Has rubbed it raw. Here children died,

But were buried elsewhere. Here discretion
Is expected of the dead. Outside the chapel
Jesus assures the lunging lorries, in a dying fall,
I am the resurrection and the life
At Easter, in late hot April.
It makes no difference. Not many birds are singing.

What resurrection for the chilled children,
Blighted and broken, bundled home to die,
Killed off between July and June,
Silent singers, aged ten, aged nine?

Flesh is finished with. Something persists
In a sister, unrelenting, stunted;
In a dead child's voice outside a midnight window
Crying *Let me in, let me in.*

Here daffodils came
And have lived to regret it. In dwarfish clumps
They glower along the verge.

Dear Mr Lee

Dear Mr Lee (Mr Smart says
it's rude to call you Laurie, but that's
how I think of you, having lived with you
really all year), Dear Mr Lee
(Laurie) I just want you to know
I used to hate English, and Mr Smart
is roughly my least favourite person,
and as for Shakespeare (we're doing him too)
I think he's a national disaster, with all those jokes
that Mr Smart has to explain why they're jokes,
and even then no one thinks they're funny,
and T. Hughes and P. Larkin and that lot
in our anthology, not exactly a laugh a minute,
pretty gloomy really, so that's why
I wanted to say Dear Laurie (sorry) your book's
the one that made up for the others, if you
could see my copy you'd know it's lived
with me, stained with Coke and KitKat
and when I had a cold, and I often
take you to bed with me to cheer me up
so Dear Laurie, I want to say sorry,
I didn't want to write a character-sketch
of your mother under headings, it seemed
wrong somehow when you'd made her so lovely,
and I didn't much like those questions
about *social welfare in the rural community*
and *the seasons as perceived by an adolescent*,
I didn't think you'd want your book
read that way, but bits of it I know by heart,
and I wish I had your uncles and your half-sisters
and lived in Slad, though Mr Smart says your view

of the class struggle is naïve, and the examiners
won't be impressed by me knowing so much by heart,
they'll be looking for terse and cogent answers
to their questions, but I'm not much good at terse and cogent,
I'd just like to be like you, not mind about being poor,
see everything bright and strange, the way you do,
and I've got the next one out of the Public Library,
about Spain, and I asked Mum about learning
to play the fiddle, but Mr Smart says Spain isn't
like that any more, it's all Timeshare villas
and Torremolinos, and how old were you
when you became a poet? (Mr Smart says for anyone
with my punctuation to consider poetry as a career
is enough to make the angels weep).

PS Dear Laurie, please don't feel guilty for
me failing the exam, it wasn't your fault,
it was mine, and Shakespeare's,
and maybe Mr Smart's, I still love *Cider*,
it hasn't made any difference.

'Very quiet here'

Picture postcard of Aldeburgh sent by Thomas Hardy to his sister, Kate Hardy, on 11 May 1912

For Bill Greenslade

In Wessex no doubt the old habits resume:
Fair maidens seduced in their innocent bloom,
May-month for suicide, and other crimes
(Two Dorchester murders discussed in *The Times*),
Mutilation of corpses, infanticide, rape,
And so many reasons for purchasing crêpe.
All stirring at home. But here vacancy reigns;
I have nothing to watch but my varicose veins.

> *Very quiet here.*
> *Not an apprentice has perished this year.*

I envy Crabbe the matter that he saw:
Those wasting ills peculiar to the poor,
Decline and dissolution, debts and duns,
The dreary marshes and the pallid suns –
So much for him to write about. And I
In Wessex homely ironies can spy.

> *None of that here.*
> *Even dear Emma a trifle less queer.*

Deck-chaired and straw-hatted I sit at my ease,
With each blighted prospect determined to please.
Inside my old skin I feel hope running on –
Perhaps a changed life when poor Emma is gone?
Strange foreknowings fret me: guns, music and war,
A corpse with no heart, a young Briton ashore
Walks here where I sit with the atheist Clodd,
Discussing the quirks of that local cult, God.

> *I ponder how*
> *Time Past and Time to Come pester me now.*

At Averham

Here my four-year-old father opened a gate,
And cows meandered through into the wrong field.

I forget who told me this. Not, I think,
My sometimes reticent father. Not much I know

About the childhood of that only child. Just
How to pronounce the name, sweetly deceitful

In its blunt spelling, and how Trent
Was his first river. Still here, but the church

Closed now, graveyard long-grassed,
No one to ask in the village. Somewhere here,

I suppose, I have a great-grandfather buried,
Of whom nothing is known but that, dying, he called

My father's mother from Kent to be forgiven.
She came, and was. And came again

To her sister, my great-aunt, for
Her dying pardon too. So my chatty mother,

But couldn't tell what needed so much forgiving,
Or such conclusive journeys to this place.

Your father, pampered only brother
Of many elder sisters, four miles away,

Grew up to scull on this river. My father,
Transplanted, grew up near poets and palaces,

Changed Trent for Thames. Water was in his blood;
In a dry part of Kent his telephone exchange

Was a river's name; he went down to die
Where Arun and Adur run out to the sea.

Your father, going north, abandoned skiffs for cars,
And lived and died on the wind-blasted North Sea shore.

They might have met, two cherished children,
Among nurses and buttercups, by the still silver Trent,

But didn't. That other implacable river, war,
Trawled them both in its heady race

Into quick-march regiments. I don't suppose they met
On any front. They found our mothers instead.

So here I stand, where ignorance begins,
In the abandoned churchyard by the river,

And think of my father, his mother, her father,
Your father, and you. Two fathers who never met,

Two daughters who did. One boy went north, one south,
Like the start of an old tale. Confusions

Of memory rise: rowing, and rumours of war,
And war, and peace; the secret in-fighting

That is called marriage. And children, children,
Born by other rivers, streaming in other directions.

You like the sound of my father. He would
Have loved you plainly, for loving me.

Reconciliation is for the quick, quickly. There isn't enough
Love yet in the world for any to run to waste.

A Wartime Education

Lessons with Mam'zelle were difficult.
Le général would crop up in the middle of
The most innocent Daudet. Tears for *la France*,
La belle France embarrassed our recitation
Of nouns with tricky plurals: hibou, chou, *hélas*, bijou.

A father in uniform conferred status. Mine,
Camping it up with the Home Guard in Kent
On summer nights, too human for heroics.

Bananas and oranges, fruit of triumphant
Decimated convoys, were amazements
Of colour and light, too beautiful to eat.
(In any case, eating three bananas
Straight off, one after the other,
Was certain death. We all knew that.)

Struggling through adolescence, trying
To accommodate Macbeth, parents, God,
Teachers of mathematics, it was hard
To sustain plain hatred for *the Hun*,

Known only as nightly whines, searchlights, thuds, bomb-sites.
Might he not, like Aeneas, have reasons
(Insufficient, but understandable) for what he did?
I found it hard to remember which side

I was on, argued endlessly at home,
Once, rashly, in a bus, and had to be defended
By mother from a war-widow. *Careless talk*
Costs lives warned the posters. I had no secrets

To offer, but acquired a habit of
Permanent secrecy, never admitted
How I hated the wolf-whistling lorry-loaded
Soldiers, passing me *en route* to D-day.

Washing-up

For Hilda Cotterill

Our mother, hater of parties and occasions,
Made much of the washing-up after. It became an exorcizing,
A celebration. Outsiders gone, the kitchen choked
With leftovers, disordered courses, mucky fiddly forks,
The alarming best glasses. She worked a system,
A competition. First we stacked the mess
In regular order: glasses, cutlery, plates
(Each in their kind); saucepans and base things last.

Then we began. She washed, I wiped; to the first to finish,
The prize of *putting-away*. A wiper-up
Should finish first. I never did, for mother
Slaved in a bacchic frenzy, scattering Vim
And purity, splashing new libations
Of suds and scalding water, piling with exquisite fingers
(Unringed for the occasion) the china in ranks,
Knives all together. I was made slow by her passion.

And as we worked she sang. My doughty mother –
Who lived through wars and took life seriously,
Never read fiction, seldom laughed at jokes –
My sorcerer-mother sang grand opera,
Parodied makeshift words and proper music.
Softly awoke her heart, without too much bathos,
But *Samso-o-o-n* got her going, and she never
Took *Trovatore* seriously: *Ah, I have sighed to rest me
Deep in the quiet grave* she'd serenade
The carving-knife, from that a short step
To saucepans and the Jewel Song: *Marguerita, this is not I.
High-born maiden I must be, high-born maiden* . . .
Her mezzo skidding along coloratura country,
My laughter rattling the stacks. The men

Came down to hear. And as she nipped
Between cupboards (having won), she added the footwork
Of humbler songs: *Home James, and don't spare*
The horses. This night has been ruin for me. Home James,
And don't spare the horses. I'm ruined as ruined can be
With a pert little mime. She liked these ruined maids,
Or about to be. *No! No! A thousand times no!*
You cannot buy my caress. No! No! A thousand times no!
I'd rather die than say yes. But her feet denied it.

Lastly, when all was done, her party-piece
True to the self she seldom let us see:
I feel so silly when the moon comes out . . .
Then, everything purged and placed, we'd go to bed.

O I remember my magical mother dancing
And singing after the party, under the airer
With the used tea towels hanging up to dry.

Learning to read you, twenty years ago,
Over the pub lunch cheese-and-onion rolls.

Learning you eat raw onions; learning your taste
For obscurity, how you encode teachers and classrooms

As *the hands, the shop-floor*; learning to hide
The sudden shining naked looks of love. And thinking

The rest of our lives, the rest of our lives
Doing perfectly ordinary things together – riding

In buses, walking in Sainsbury's, sitting
In pubs eating cheese-and-onion rolls,

All those tomorrows. Now, twenty years after,
We've had seventy-three hundred of them, and

(If your arithmetic's right, and our luck) we may
Fairly reckon on seventy-three hundred more.

I hold them crammed in my arms, colossal crops
Of shining tomorrows that may never happen,

But may they! Still learning to read you,
To hear what it is you're saying, to master the code.

Old Man, Old Man

He lives in a world of small recalcitrant
Things in bottles, with tacky labels. He was always
A man who did-it-himself.

Now his hands shamble among clues
He left for himself when he saw better,
And small things distress: *I've lost the hammer*.

Lifelong adjuster of environments,
Lord once of shed, garage and garden,
Each with its proper complement of tackle,

World authority on twelve different
Sorts of glue, connoisseur of nuts
And bolts, not good with daughters

But a dab hand with the Black and Decker,
Self-demoted in your nineties to washing-up
After supper, and missing crusted streaks

Of food on plates; have you forgotten
The jokes you no longer tell, as you forget
If you've smoked your timetabled cigarette?

Now television has no power to arouse
Your surliness; your wife could replace on the walls
Those pictures of disinherited children,

And you wouldn't know. Now you ramble
In your talk around London districts, fretting
At how to find your way from Holborn to Soho,

And where is Drury Lane? Old man, old man,
So obdurate in your contracted world,
Living in almost-dark, *I can see you*,

You said to me, *but only as a cloud*.
When I left, you tried not to cry. I love
Your helplessness, you who hate being helpless.

Let me find your hammer. Let me
Walk with you to Drury Lane. I am only a cloud.

Looking for Jorvik

Veterans swap yarns about how long they queued
In the rain to see Tutankhamun.

Sweet summer York is nothing. They dip alertly
Into the dark, the time capsule. (*No dogs,*

Smoking, ice-cream, cameras.) History
Breathes them in, past *Pack up your troubles,*

Puffing billies, factory acts, perukes, Marston Moor,
(*Have you got a sweety, Geoffrey love?*)

Mendicant friars, the Black Death, through the one
Date everybody knows, to the ancestral

Mutter and reek. This is then, now. We are
Where it was, it is. (*There's a man as big*

As a troll at the door.) Here the foundations are,
Pit, mud, stumps, the endless tons of bone,

Tiny dark plum stones of Viking York.
(And he said *I dabbled my blade in*

Bloodaxe's boy.) At this level the appalling
Icelander Egil who must not be killed at night

(*Night-killings are murder*) saved his neck by his
Head-Ransom song next day. And got off.

As we do, in the souvenir shop. *That wouldn't
Interest me. But for someone like Barbara,*

*Who's a real intellectual . . . She was an English teacher,
You know.* T-shirts, baseball caps, keyrings, tapestry kits,

Activity packs proclaim *Eric Bloodaxe Rules OK*. And I
Have unearthed my own past under Jorvik's shaft,

Changing trains twenty years ago on York station at midnight
Among kit-bagged soldiers, on my way to you, thinking
   suddenly:

I am on my way to life.

In 948, Egil had been shipwrecked off the Yorkshire coast, and
knew he could expect no mercy from Eric Bloodaxe, who ruled
York, because he had killed Eric's son. The rules of that society
prevented Eric from having Egil put to death at once, because he
had arrived after dark, so Egil was given the chance of composing
overnight his Head-Ransom song (twenty stanzas in praise of Eric).
This, because it was so brilliant, forced Eric to grant Egil his life.

Homing In

Somewhere overseas England are struggling
On a sticky wicket; somewhere in Europe
An elder statesman is dying *adagio*; and here,
Nowhere precisely, I slip to pips and bens
Through the occupied air.

Somewhere along this road an invisible ditch
Signals tribe's end, an important mutation of [ʌ];
Somewhere among these implacable place-names
People are living coherent lives. For me the unfocused
Landscape of exile.

Somewhere along this watershed, weather
Will assert itself, swap wet for dry,
Scribble or flare on windscreens, send freak gusts
Sneaking round juggernauts, ravel traffic with
A long foggy finger.

Home starts at Birmingham. Places
Where I have walked are my auguries:
The stagey Malverns, watery sharp Bredon,
May Hill's arboreal quiff. These as I pass
Will bring me luck if they look my way.

I should be rehearsing contingencies,
Making resolutions, allowing for change
In the tricky minor modes of love. But,
Absorbed by nearly-home names,
Dear absurd Saul, Framilode, Frampton-on-Severn,

I drop, unprepared, into one particular
Parish, one street, one house, one you,
Exact, ignorant and faithful as swallows commuting
From Sahara to garage shelf.

Teacher's Christmas

It's not so much the ones whose cards don't come,
Friends of one's parents, old distinguished colleagues
Who taught the colonies and, retiring home,
Did a spot of dignified coaching. Their sudden silence
Is a well-bred withdrawing, not unexpected.

But those who move from address to more sheltered address,
Whose writing gutters gently year by year,
Whose *still hoping to see you again* after *love*
Is bluff; or those who write after Christmas
Because *cards are so expensive now*. Ah those, how those

Punctiliously chart their long decline.

The stages grow familiar, like disease.
First it's *my dauntless Mini, less staunch now,*
But I could come by bus, with sandwiches.
I shall enjoy the jaunt.

WEA classes go. Then television
Becomes remote, and radio's
Hard for the hard of hearing. Still they write,
They write at Christmas. Prithee, good death's-heads,
Bid me not remember mine end.

Season as well of cards from brilliant girls,
A little less incisive every year,
Reporting comings, goings: another Hannah,
Another Jamie; another husband going off; and
Writing my thesis is like digging a well with a pin.

You, the storm-troopers of a newer, better world.

Down with you, holly. Come down, ivy.

CHRONICLE (UNFINISHED)

For Mick North and Janni Howker

1. *1938*

A slack year on the estate, the men
Hanging about idle. Mrs Pretty set them
To dig the heathy tumps outside the garden.

    In this year the Germans marched
    Into Austria, and they held it.

Basil, the one with the gift, *had a profound feeling*
(Says authority) *for the local soil.* Grew wedded to it.
If e'd ad is bed (says gardener Jack), *e'd ave slept
Out there in the trench.*

    In this year also wise rulers in Europe
    Met at Munich and spoke for peace.

Three mounds opened. Strange things found
In a boatgrave. *I was a green hand*
(Says Jack), *didn't rightly understand
The value of the things.*

2. *1939*

    In this year Adolf the leader sent men
    Into Bohemia, and they held it.

They trenched the highest barrow, found
The bows of a great ship. Experts came,
Under the darkening skies of the world, to see
What hid at Sutton Hoo.

In this year also the men of Italy
Marched into Albania, and they held it.

The archaeologist spoke. *We might
As well have a bash* (said he, being young),
So a bash was what we had.

In the Bull pub at Woodbridge they stayed,
Clever, lanky young men with prewar haircuts;
Eminent, emeritus now, with their pasts behind them,
Retired, superseded, dead. And the gold
Came out of the earth bright and shining
As the day it went in.

In this year also Adolf the leader
And Benedict the leader swore to keep faith.
Men called it the pact of steel.

The winds of that year blew Redwald's flaked bones
Over the fields of his kingdom. Gold leaf also
Floated away in that weather.

Potent treasures were packed in boxes and tins
Scrounged from chemists and grocers. It was all borne
From the great ship by an elderly Ford
Which ran out of petrol outside the gates
Of the British Museum.

In this year also the men of Russia swore
That they would not fight against the Germans.
Both sides set their hands to it.

Learned clerks counted and cosseted
The awesome things, and they were stacked
In Aldwych underground for the duration.

In this year also the men of Germany
Marched into Poland, and they held it.
Then the rulers of England and France,

Who were handfast, defied the Germans,
    And there was open war.

Long enough ago.

Now Mrs Pretty is dead, who loyally gave
The royal lot to the nation. Gardener Jack
And brown-fingered Basil died too, no doubt;
We have no records of them. But high to this day
In Londonchester looms the High King's regalia,
Sword, sceptre, shield, helm, drinking horns and harp,
Patched and polished, explained, made innocent, aimless.

Behind glass, air-conditioned, they wait in their own way
For what comes next:
                    another inhumation?
                                another finding?
                                        another year?

The Comforters

For Philip Gross

The night cometh, when no man can work – John 9:4

Because their aim was not comfort, these
Are the comforters. That we find comfort
In what they wrote is our affair,
Not theirs. They never imagined immortality,
But watched each minute instant so hard
That it broke and flowered into ever.

Samuel of London, Gilbert of Selborne,
Francis of Clyro. And many more. Their own lives
By no means easy. We could tell them
The last dates in those diaries,
The hard labour of their dying: *a nest*
Of no less than seven stones in the left kidney;
A nervous cough and a wandering gout;
Peritonitis on a delayed, delightful
Honeymoon, aged thirty-nine.

                We prize them
Not for their ends, but for the light
Of their everlasting present. Like them, we wait
For our own particular doomsday. Ours
May be premature, comprehensive. In the meantime, they
Reach down centuries with their accidental
Offer of comfort.

              So I choose to believe
The old lie: that we all died normally
Ever after: *suddenly, following*
A road accident; after a long illness
Patiently borne. Not in the monstrous
Nuclear glare, but in the moderate

Darkness and light, darkness and light
That were the evening and the morning
Of the first ever day.

Costa Geriatrica

Evening quarters; land
Of the tranquil solo deckchair,
Of the early Ovaltine nightcap.

Here patient shop-assistants
Pick the right change from freckled
Trembling hands, and wrap

Single rashers tenderly. Here gardening
Is dangerous as bull-fights.
Dogs are dwarfish,

Coddled and lethal.
Here sagas are recited
Of long-dead husbands,

Varicose veins, comforting ministers,
Scarcity of large-print library books,
And endless hands of photographs

Of the happily-ever-after children
They make believe they have:
A nice son in the police force

And two lovely children.
Marriages are made in heaven,
For Mr Right not only exists

But arrives on cue. Tragedy
Is reduced to a foot-note: *The husband?*
Oh, he went wrong, or died,

Or something. They have all
Had what they wanted:
A lovely little square family,

And now, comforting morticians:
That's the man I want at my funeral,
If anything ever happens to me.

Superannuated Psychiatrist

Old scallywag scapegoat has skedaddled,
Retired at last to bridge and both kinds of bird-watching.
No more suspect phone calls from shady acquaintances,
Anonymous ladies and flush-faced Rotarians.

He could always be blamed when case-notes strayed.
(His MG boot? His mistress's bed? We enjoyed guessing.)
How we shall miss his reliable shiftiness,
Wow and flutter on tape, Wimbledon-fortnight illness,

Dr Macavity life. Dear foxy quack,
I relished your idleness, your improvisations,
Your faith in my powers of you-preservation.
Who will shoulder our errors now?

What of your replacement, the new high-flyer,
Smelling of aftershave and ambition? Is that tic
Telling us something his mind will arrive at later?
Meantime, I watch his parentheses. A man so much given

To brackets is hedging his bets.

Reception in Bristol

These men are rich; they buy
Pictures before asking prices.

Their shirts are exquisite; I know instinctively
I must not say so.

Conversations are precisely timed,
Costing so much per word per minute.

Wives are worn small this year, soberly dressed.
Their eyes are wild, but there is no exit.

Schools that encourage music, says the chairman,
Have no hooligans. No one replies.

The photographer is our *memento mori*.
He takes two sandwiches at once

From the curtseying waitress. There is a crumb
At the corner of his mouth, and he has

To go on somewhere else. He is here to remind us
That in this city Savage died, a prisoner;

That Chatterton poisoned himself in his London garret
Rather than creep back here.

Titania to Bottom

For Alistair and Becky

You had all the best lines. I
Was the butt, too immortal
To be taken seriously. I don't grudge you
That understated donkey dignity.
It belongs to your condition. Only,
Privately, you should know my passion
Wasn't the hallucination they imagined,
Meddling king and sniggering fairy.

You, Bottom, are what I love. That nose,
Supple, aware; that muzzle, planted out
With stiff, scratchable hairs; those ears,
Lofty as bulrushes, smelling of hay harvest,
Twitching to each subtle electric
Flutter of the brain! Oberon's loving
Was like eating myself – appropriate,
Tasteless, rather debilitating.

But holding you I held the whole
Perishable world, rainfall and nightjar,
Tides, excrement, dandelions, the first foot,
The last pint, high blood pressure, accident, prose.

The sad mechanical drone of enchantment
Finished my dream. I knew what was proper,
Reverted to fairyland's style.

                    But Bottom, Bottom,
How I shook to the shuffle of your mortal heart.

Neck-Verse

Armour of phrase disarms despair;
Ancestral patchwork plasters. Someone else
Was wounded here and stitched a turn to fit
The later maimed. I cherish
A cat's cradle of country proverbs,
Homely as singin' hinnies, handy as hankies.
Not hard equivocal wisdom for grand folk,
But reassuring halloos from the past:
We have been here before you, pet!

My kitchen prescriptions:
For Resignation:
You can't get feathers off the cat.

To take the ache out of Age:
He's seen a few Easter Sundays.

For the different ways menfolk are difficult:
Cross-grained: *He's got his braces twisted.*
Stingy: *He'd kill a louse for the hide and tallow.*
Impossible, like mine: *Awkward as Dick's hatband.*
*Went three times round the crown
And wouldn't tie a bow.*

Hysteria has many cues; its bubble
Needs pricking. After Effort:
It's all over now, and the child's name's Anthony.
To bypass weepy Thanks: *That'll be ninepence,*
Or *Keep your seats, there's no collection.*

For Last Ditch Stands: *That's me,*
And my dog's at Tow Law.

And O, for how it should be, could have been,
I have two simples: *As easy*
As me granny's old shoe, and
All in together, like the folks at Shields.

Too often, though, just the longing
For freedom, a fresh start:
I wish I was married and living at Jarrow.

I know what they'll say of me: *She brought*
Her pigs to a poor market in the end. Yes,
That'll be what it'll be. And to comfort me,
Cheer up, hinny, it's nobody's neck.

But that's not true. It is some body's neck.
It's mine.

Neck-Verse: The first verse of Psalm 51, so called because it was the
trial verse of those who claimed Benefit of Clergy. If a condemned
person was able to read this verse (thus originally showing that he
was ordained, and therefore exempt from trial by a secular court), he
had saved his neck. This privilege was later extended to anyone who
could read and write, or even who knew the psalm's first verse by
heart. It was abolished in 1827.

Awkward Subject

The light is wonderful, he says. Not light
For house-agents, certainly. They avoid
November shots, when wisped and bony trees
Throw a disturbing shade on property.

Stand there. Just a bit further. Don't look at the dog.
My casual adaptation to the place
(One hand in pocket, right knee slightly bent)
May not be what I mean, but is in danger
Of immortality.

                I feel my teeth support me
Against my inner lip; face him with all my skin.
Sensing my misery, *Would you rather smile?*
He asks. And break the lens, I hope. Words are my element.
Photograph them.

The Room Where Everyone Goes

Mount Grace Priory

God's humour: uncouth helmet of silence;
God's blessing: hard cold water;
God's nursery: frigid stone.

His curriculum: spinning wheel; loom;
The word; and God, fidgety partner,
Fills the cell, or vacates it, at a whim.

Here we come, the inheritors, girt about with guidebooks.
Fast, prayer, solitude, face us like whips.
We try to imagine foot's curt patrol
Down each midget cloister; garden breath
Of mint and chives; the dished up smell
Of dinner the lay-brother left in the dog-leg hatch;
Holy sting of Latin in cold teeth
On dark mornings. Here, the monk's chair and bed,
Where we can sit, or lie. Here, his window;
We can look out of it. How alien it all seems,
But for one spot, in the north wall,
At the end of the covered way. – *Ooh, look!*
The loo/the toilet/the bog! We run to see,
Take turns at sitting, feel (of course) at home.

Such cold, clean men.

The King's curriculum: ten monks from the London house
Chained hand and foot to Newgate posts
And left to rot (*Despatched by the hand of God,*
Said a careful cleric). Daily, a woman bribed her way in
With a bucket of meat, and fed them like fledglings;
(*Which having done, she afterwards took from them*
Their natural filth). In the end the gaoler panicked,
In the end (of course) they died.

They were always on sentry-go, never on leave.
Drill, practice, training never stopped.
One way or other, they knew, God's inspection was coming.

They are out of reach. We can walk where they did,
But the guts and the goodness are beyond us.

Cold and godliness alienate.
The scent of the commonplace brings them home.

The Room Where Everyone Goes: I've borrowed this from W. H. Auden's 'The Geography of the House':

> . . . this white-tiled cabin
> Arabs call *The House where*
> *Everybody goes.*

The London house: i.e., the London Charterhouse, founded in 1371, suppressed in 1538.
a woman: Margaret Clement (née Gigs), adopted daughter of Sir Thomas More. When she was prevented, she climbed to the roof and tried to let food down in a basket.

Counting Song

One man and his dog
Went to mow a meadow.

Not always the same dog,
But the man looks the same, disposable,
Scrapped. Hungerford Bridge his meadow.

This is the city we come to when we're young,
With the golden pavements. Where office-workers whisk
Like weir-water over zebras; where 15s and 77s
Snuffle down bus lanes, showy as heralds.

One woman and a baby

Probably borrowed, we say, not looking,
Moving on. We need to move on.
Our shoes are embarrassed. Our shoes are what she sees.

There's less of sky, now the great Lego thumbs
Angle their vacant heads into the gullspace,
But the saints watch us, Martin the beggars' friend,
Bride in her wedding-cake hat, and Paul,
Skywise and circumspect, sitting out centuries
Under his helmet, Thames washing past,
Refusing to run softly.

One gran and her bottle
Have given up on mowing.

These are waste people, grazing in litterbins,
Sleeping in cardboard, swaddled in broadsheets
And Waitrose plastic bags, who will not be recycled,
Must lie where they fall.
These are the heirs, the true Londoners,

Who work in this stern meadow. The others
Are on their way to somewhere else:
Statesmen and filmstars, remote, chauffeur-driven;
Volatile journalists, folding themselves in taxis,
As homegoers fold themselves into introspection
And the *Evening Standard*.

Written on Hungerford Bridge in letters of chalk:
Save Our Earth. Save Twyford Down.

Save Earth. Save Twyford Down. Save every one.

A Major Road for Romney Marsh

It is a kingdom, a continent.
Nowhere is like it.

> (Ripe for development)

It is salt, solitude, strangeness.
It is ditches, and windcurled sheep.
It is sky over sky after sky.

> (It wants hard shoulders,
> Happy Eaters,
> Heavy breathing of HGVs)

It is obstinate hermit trees.
It is small, truculent churches
Huddling under the gale force.

> (It wants WCs, Kwiksaves,
> Artics, Ind Ests, Jnctns)

It is the Military Canal
Minding its peaceable business,
Between the Levels and the Marsh.

> (It wants INVESTING IN ROADS,
> Sgns sying T'DEN, F'STONE,
> C'BURY)

It is itself, and different.

> (Nt fr lng. Nt fr lng.)

Odysseus' Cat

For Barbara Britton

Aged and broken, prostrate on the ground,
Neglected Argus lies, once fabled hound.
Odysseus' footsteps he alone descries,
Perceives the master through the slave's disguise;
He lifts his head, and wags his tail, and dies.

– *The Corgiad*, trans. J.G.C.

     Not that I don't believe
The first part of the yarn – the ten years' war.
Ten seems quite modest for a genocide.
No, it's the ten years' journey afterwards
I boggle at, bearing in mind
The undemanding nature of the route.
Why did he take so long? One thing's for sure –
Those junkies, cannibals, one-eyed aliens,
And friendly ladies living alone on islands –
Well, what do you think? Of course. Exactly.

In the meantime, in another part of the archipelago,
Old Argus had been catsmeat long before.
Man's best wears out, with rushing around and barking,
And digging and wagging. Cats, on the contrary, last:
The harmonious posture, exact napping,
Judicious absences from home . . .
       I had, of course,
Been busy. Did what I could to discourage
The mistress's unappealing Don Juans,
Lurked boldly in dark corners, slashing
Shins of passers-by; performed
Uninhibited glissades down dinner tables,
Scattering wine and olives; free fell
From rafters upon undefended necks;

Produced well-timed vomit in my lady's chamber
When a gallant went too far; and I helped
With demolishing the tapestry each night,
Having an inbred talent.

So when Odysseus came, I rubbed his legs.
He recognized me – well, he said, *Puss, puss*,
Which is all you learn to expect.
                              And then the liar
Concocts this monstrous calumny of me:
He leaves me out, supplants me with a dog,
A dead dog, too. And the one thing
Everyone believes is that dog's tale,
Tale of the faithful hound.
                        You'll see
I've improved his version; cut out the lies,
The sex, the violence. Poor old Argus
Wouldn't have known the difference. But cats
Are civilized. I thought you'd see it my way.

On Worms, and Being Lucky

Two kinds of sand. One heavy, gritty,
That falters moodily under your toes, like custard;
The other, shiny weedy ribs, and further,

Out of sight, the standstill sea. You tramp along
In sunbonnet and spade, summer's regalia.
You choose a grey snake's nest, slice into it,

And yes, there *are* lugworms, and you carve them out,
And he hoicks you up, your dad, to the space round his head.
You've got the knack, my princess, he says. *You're lucky.*

Then there's your turn for betting. Bored by favourites,
You always picked the unfancied outsider.
The field foundered at Becher's. Or something.

Anyway, yours won, against the odds
(*Lucky, my princess!*) since you knew it would,
And knew it into winning (*Sweetheart. Lucky*).

After the operation, you were sent for.
(He was propped up in bed, reeking of ether,
Possibly dying.) You held the big limp hands,

And lugged him back to life, like a cow from a bog.
He clung to your luck, and kept it
For two more years. You gave him something,
Not knowing what it was. (*The knack*, he wheezes.)

Or love, maybe. Two kinds of luck.
My luck, dear father, flashy and absurd,
A matter of long odds and stop-press news;

Yours was the gift that sees life gold side up,
So that a knack of finding worms becomes
A serious blessing.

What, in Our House?

'The play [*Macbeth*] is remarkably short, and it may be there has been some cutting.' Here is a tentatively restored fragment of Act II, Scene iii.

MACDUFF   O Banquo, Banquo,
Our royal master's murdered.

LADY MACBETH   Woe, alas!
What, in our house?

BANQUO   Too cruel anywhere.

LADY MACBETH   That's not the point. Who cares for anywhere?
Mere woolly-minded liberals. But *here*
Is where I am, my house, my place, my world,
My fortress against time and dirt and things.
Here I deploy my garrison of soap,
And, like all housewives, just about contrive
To outmanoeuvre chaos. Not a job
For men. What man alive will grovel
Scrubbing at floorboards to mop up the blood?
(No doubt there's blood? Or if not, sick or shit
Or other filth that women have to handle?)

BANQUO   O gentle lady . . .

LADY MACBETH   Only women know
The quantity of blood there is that waits
To flood from bodies; how it soaks and seeps
In wood and wool and walls, and stains for ever.
No disinfectant, I can tell you, Banquo,
So strong as blood. Then, the implicit slur
Upon my hospitality. Was Duncan
Suffocated? Something wrong with the pillows!
Was his throat cut? Check the carving knives!
Poison? Blame the cuisine. I wish to heaven,
Banquo, he'd died in *your* house. Your wife
Would tell you how I feel.

DONALBAIN   What is amiss?
MACDUFF   Your royal father's murdered.
MALCOLM   O, by whom?
LADY MACBETH   Such donnish syntax at so grave a moment!
                How hard to frame the first and random thought
                Detection snuffs at, to seem innocent
                And psycholinguistically correct at once.
                And my *best* bedroom too.

DNA

'. . . and so their horses went where they would.'
– Malory, *Le Morte d'Arthur*, Book XXI, Chapter X

So at the end the company dissolved.
Kings died. Queens turned into nuns.
Knights came to grief, or left in symbolic boats.
They made Lancelot a priest. And those other knights
Read holy books, and holp for to sing mass,
And tinkled little bells. Then it was over.

Their horses, the noble destriers,
The lordly ones, plaited and groomed and oiled,
With their grave names and their alarming harness,
Who carried nothing, except men to war,
Stepped mildly over the brambles, tasted grass,
Cantered composedly through the forest waste
Of early England, and at last
Went where they liked, quick and shining
Through kingdoms. Time whittled them down.
They became the dwarfish ponies of now,
Shaggy and hungry, living on the edge.

Sometimes, in a foal's crest, you can see
Some long-extinguished breeding. So in us,
The high-rise people and the dispossessed,
The telly idols, fat men in fast cars,
Something sometimes reverts to the fine dangerous strain
Of Galahad the high prince, Lancelot the undefeated,
Arthur the king.

Collateral Damage

The minor diplomat who brings terms for a ceasefire
Enters through a side-door, in the small hours,
Wearing a belted raincoat.

The children have become bold. At the first siren
They cried, and ran for their mothers.
Now they are worldly-wise,

They clamour to watch dogfights above the house,
They prefer under-the-kitchen-table to the shelter,
They play fighting games

Of reading the paper by bomblight,
Pretending to be the enemy. These children
Are no longer safe.

They have learned rash and contrary for ever. Come soon,
O minor diplomat in the belted raincoat, come
To capitulate. For the children have ack-ack nerves,
And a landmine has fallen next door.

Under the reservoir, under the wind-figured water,
Are the walls, the church, the houses,
The small human things,

That in drought rise up gaunt and dripping,
And it was once Mardale, both is and is not Mardale,
But is still there,

Like the diplomat, and the crazy fearless children
Who progress through their proper stages, and the churchbells
With their nightly riddles,

And the diplomat, and the children still running
Away from shelter, into the path of the bomb.

Elma Mitchell

Thoughts after Ruskin

Women reminded him of lilies and roses.
Me they remind rather of blood and soap,
Armed with a warm rag, assaulting noses,
Ears, neck, mouth and all the secret places:

Armed with a sharp knife, cutting up liver,
Holding hearts to bleed under a running tap,
Gutting and stuffing, pickling and preserving,
Scalding, blanching, broiling, pulverising,
– All the terrible chemistry of their kitchens.

Their distant husbands lean across mahogany
And delicately manipulate the market,
While safe at home, the tender and the gentle
Are killing tiny mice, dead snap by the neck,
Asphyxiating flies, evicting spiders,
Scrubbing, scouring aloud, disturbing cupboards,
Committing things to dustbins, twisting, wringing,
Wrists red and knuckles white and fingers puckered,
Pulpy, tepid. Steering screaming cleaners
Around the snags of furniture, they straighten
And haul out sheets from under the incontinent
And heavy old, stoop to importunate young,
Tugging, folding, tucking, zipping, buttoning,
Spooning in food, encouraging excretion,
Mopping up vomit, stabbing cloth with needles,
Contorting wool around their knitting needles,
Creating snug and comfy on their needles.

Their huge hands! their everywhere eyes! their voices
Raised to convey across the hullabaloo,
Their massive thighs and breasts dispensing comfort,

Their bloody passages and hairy crannies,
Their wombs that pocket a man upside down!

And when all's over, off with overalls,
Quickly consulting clocks, they go upstairs,
Sit and sigh a little, brushing hair,
And somehow find, in mirrors, colours, odours,
Their essences of lilies and of roses.

The Corset

The corset came today. I cannot wear it.

What are your difficulties, may I ask?
A slight constriction round about the heart?
That, at your time of life, you must expect,
The back and shoulders mainly take the weight,
Astonishingly comfortable, on the whole
And really very stylish, – for your size.
This line is very flattering to the bust,
And this delineates what was once a waist,
And further down, you see, complete control . . .

You'll soon acquire the knack; just slip it on,
Wriggle, distort, contract – that's right, that's it.
Now you are one smooth mould from head to thighs.
You'll be surprised how good it makes you feel . . .

The corset came today. I will not wear it.
Come, lumpish lumbering muscles, to your task,
Unsupple wits, turn sinuous again,
Or live as limp and cripple, but let live.

Alice Uglier

Alice is uglier now by several years.
    Her eyes
Are sunk and fortified against surprise,
    Humiliations, tears.
Sensible to the bone, her gait proclaims.
    Her cut
Of coat disdains the sympathizer, but
    Her mouth is restless: tensions dug
    These trenches in her throat.

She wasn't bred on love or promises,
    Lonely, never alone,
Her future was provided for, not cherished.
    She nursed
Her nearest through senility and worse.
    Placid in gratitude, dumb to abuse,
    She kept
The business out of debt, the books in order,
    But now, it seems, the monkey's loose,
And something's tearing papers in the cellar
    Far down.

While habit, like a well-maintained machine,
    Keeps up the play of knife and fork
And answers questions in between –
    Her sturdy tree is withered to a rod.
She's given up her country walks,
    (Too stiff to stoop for primroses)
Under the table, foot and fist
    Tap out their private messages –
She wakes in darkness to her bath of flames
    And wonders what became of God.

Still
She must get back, or she'll be missed
   Over the coffee, she'll insist
We should go fifty-fifty on the bill.
This is a block that salts will not remove.
   I pour out coffee, and retain
Her drowning image, and my useless love.

Hanging Out the Wash

Our garments, air-inflated, big with wind,
Dance their caricatures on the flogging line.

The teeth of wooden and plastic pegs hold down
Our woollies to be raped by a screaming north-easter.
The sun assaults their colouring: a shirt
Is crucified in ice: knickers distended, pregnant.

Strung
Between house and garden,
Tied
To a sagging, flapping line

They are caricatures – oh, surely!

Look, it's beginning to rain, I must bring them in
Till, warm and dry and tame, they fit us again.

Winter in Lodgings

Mr Pritchard was the first to pass away.
Out late, wet, and got the pneumonia
On the top of his bronchitis,
In all that cold he reached a high temperature
And was cremated, last January.
They put the remains in a very nice little jar
But nobody quite seems to know just whereabouts it is.
They say he was just a wee bit too fond of the bottle,
Poor soul, in a jar, pickled at last.

Mrs Ledbury, she was more romantic,
She had everything fixed up,
She was laid to rest in peace in her native village,
She lies in the Midland clay beside the by-pass
Motionless, without her knitting-needles.
Strangers can now go past her unidentified,
The telly has lost the spice of her disapproval,
We no longer know what she thinks about simply everything.

Miss Kelly is one of a number in North London.
We mean to go up and find her and take some flowers
On a fine Sunday in summer,
For she was nice, Miss Kelly, and fond of flowers
And babies and kittens and calendars. We hope Heaven
Will be just what she fancied. Killed by a motor-bike.
Not a very nice death for a ladylike person.

With Mr Wilson, it was Anno Domini,
And took much longer.
Doing his crossword puzzles up to the last
He began to find the clues a little beyond him,
Never mind, he said, we'll get the solution tomorrow,

Which he finally did.
                         Yes, it's been quite a winter,
To think about, over the evening cocoa,
With a kind of satisfaction.

Late Fall

About the height of noon
The manless creatures come to take the sun.
This one we call a butterfly
Has landed on my hand, I don't know why.

Some warmth or texture or suspected sap
Inveigled it into this possible trap.

Top-heavy: ticklish; nourished on a weed,
Dotted and dashed with signals I can't read,

It comes in black, white, orange, blue and brown,
Topples a moment and settles blandly down.

Calm in the sun that made today its day.

Be off, you.
Do whatever it is you have to do,

I do not kill, nor spare, nor pardon.
There is no god walking in this garden.

The Last of the Rain

The rain has almost stopped; and still the drops
Ping and smack from the edge of the soused thatch,
Water dawdles and maunders in the channels
Of the wrinkling road, and all the unsettled hill
Strains at ditches, fuddles in gutters, erupts
In sudden springs, and sticks in the straight throat
Of grating and drain, a timid humus of weed,
Leavings of green; slime; and kneeling straws
Sucked from the stubble; somersaulted twigs,
Bark, husk, rubble and dust now water-winged,
Voluble, sociable now in the fluent flood.

Wellington and galosh, tyre-splash and hoof
Pock and print the various mobile mud,
But the sliding wile of silt
Drips back into its rut, and there sinks;
Detritus droops; sand settles; the murky clears;
And all the turbid rush
Takes on tranquillity, and holds the sky
Shining, in water colour,
Calmly reflects the jewelled intangible air
On an undercoat of mud, as the earth must,
Stretched as it is on the determining rocks
From face of clay to queer unvisited core;
Whatever opaque impasto swirls above
– Alive in stench and daub, slither and crunch,
Worm, bacteria, weed-seed, harvest-seed –
The centre's drab and hard.

The superficial rain dances and sings,
Sobers and steadies, seeps and carries on down
To manufacture coal-and-diamond stuff
Or sharpen rot, where only darkness is

And carcases, and promises
That make men mine the pit, and die of the dead weight
Of earth and water mixed.
Rivers run underground, as waters can,
Where wits trip and the will chills and the mere throat
Falters and chokes; the centre has no voice.

The superficial rain dances and sings
And so do I, do I, do I. Do I?
The centre has no voice.

The cows come close to the house
Heavy with milk and rain,
Breathing out moist reproaches, shuffling muck,
On the wrong cold side of the wall where warm and dry
I
Sit at a desk and write the praise of wet
In the blood's decline, while the running of the rain
Stops, perhaps permanently. Anyhow, stops.

Turning Out the Mattresses

When we were turning out the mattresses,
Fooling and laughing and heaving and calling across,
I suddenly remembered: you aren't here.
And stood, shaken to pieces by the loss;
As we were turning out the mattresses,
I had to go on. Irreparable distresses,
Eloquent elegies, the waste of tears
Aren't for women with supper to get and all.
It was only a year ago, the funeral
To the time of turning out the mattresses.

This bit of paper's your memorial.

At First, My Daughter

She is world without understanding.
She is made of sound.
She drinks me.

We laugh when I lift her by the feet.
She is new as a petal.
Water comes out of her mouth and her little crotch.

She gives the crook of my arm
A weight of delight.
I stare in her moving mirror of untouched flesh.

Absurd, but verifiable,
These words – mother, daughter –
They taste of receiving and relinquishing.

She will never again be quite so novel and lovely
Nor I so astonished.
In touch, we are celebrating

The first and last moments
Of being together and separate
Indissolute – till we are split

By time, and growth, and man,
The things I made her with.

Mother, Dear Mother

She is invigilator; her name is knife.
She changes nappies and sleeps in my father's bed.

If I cry blazes or trickle, she'll come to my whistle
And give me her breast. Or let me lie and cry.

Half of her's mine, and half is my hot fat father's.
To each, one arm, one eye – and then what?

What is the good of possessing half a woman?
I'll pull her down to me by her swinging hair

And eat her all up, moon-face, belly and toes,
And throw the skin to my father, to keep him warm.

Vulnerable

Everything is vulnerable at sunrise.
Houses are blurred at the edge by the creeping light.
They are not yet upright, not yet property.

Inside the houses
Bodies and beds are still to be disentangled,
Naked, bearded, sheeted, flowing, breathing,
With no cosmetic except the morning's colouring.

No body has had time to put on its uniform
To arm itself with the safe and usual phrases,
To start counting, considering, feeling hungry,
Being man or woman . . .

They lie scattered, invisible, soft, lovable,
Under the surreptitious hands of the sunrise,
The touching light.

They are not yet upright, not yet property.

Cook Speaks

I peel my hands –
(It is a habit)
Turnip hands
Fingered with carrots.

I am ribbed with celery,
Eyed with raisins,
Lipped with cherries.
I spill the beans.

Blood passes
Between my fingers
And milk, and water
And wine and spices.

Soft as flour
My sifted belly.
Salt and sugar
Heap my breasts.

I am no more beautiful
Than crackling pork
Or a skinned rabbit

But I taste good.

Recreation

She makes embroidery
As bees make honey
From flowers and colours.

It absorbs her.
She is drawn by threads
Into the heart of the pattern.

In the slipping, bitty
Ripples of domesticity
She likes the sedentary

Intricate necessity
Of this embroidery.
It must be just so, exactly,

And yet can wait, not spoiling,
Not boiling over, when
She lays it down (for cries

Of children, phone, kettle).
She rises, goes
To do whatever she has to

And returns to the quiet tugging
Of thread, unbroken,
Piecing together (when she has a moment)

Complete, unwithering roses.

Propitiation

He always apologized to statues
And sometimes to furniture, when he bumped into it.
He felt no superiority to insects
But removed them carefully from kitchen surfaces.

He sat at the wheel of a car,
Thinking of a world without predators
Or generals.
        A moment's absentmindedness –
A child on a bicycle died.

No, no, it didn't. It never happened.
But he lived all his life with this catastrophe
In imagination, as he ferried his insects
To places of safety, and apologized to statues.

How Was It Up There?

No, no,
Of course I'm not disappointed.

It was wonderful.
You were wonderful.

I know the courage
Of such a voyage,
The nervous jokes between colleagues
Who know each other like enemies.

I know
The intelligence of instruments

And the expense –
All your youth
Magnetized hard against these moments,
Released only by achievement.

I appreciate the presents you brought me back –
The stones, and the interesting
Samples of dust.

It's out of this world.
So why am I crying?

I'm crying for the moon,
That's what I'm crying for,

Your stark monopoly
And your unshared
Extra-terrestrial affair.

It's wonderful, of course.

It lies between us like a white divorce.

Wonderful

For thirty pensionable years, a walking will.

She went through problems like a reaper-and-binder
Working at speed against a break in the weather
Tidily, accurately. Her advice was excellent
But not comforting. She made decisions
With a craftsman's confidence, good days and bad,
And wore stoicism like well-cut clothes.

In church, she sang about frailty, but had no truck with it.

She kept a budgerigar (her only concession
To the fidgety unreasonable world of nature)
In a cage of course; and taught it to speak polite
Grammatical English.
                         She was unbudgeable,
Built to last – and never countenanced
Our mobile homes, collapsible marriages
And drip-dry tears.
                         Her toughest condemnation
Soft, soppy, sloppy – a schoolgirl tongue
Cutting unwieldy emotions down to size.

When time leaned against her, she took it in hand
With plans for the posthumous disposal of everything
And everyone. She foresaw the foreseeable future,
Dared it to get away with it, and died
At ninety-plus.
                         She made me feel old.

Life-cycle of the Moth*

Peach-blossom, muslin. Sallow kitten,
Gipsy.

Dark tussock, satin carpet.
Wood-leopard, scarlet tiger!

Great prominent,
Iron prominent –
Dark crimson underwing.

Emperor, white ermine,
Large emerald.

December. Frosted green.
Lackey, red-necked footman.
Drinker.
Scarce silver.

Old lady,
Figure of eighty,
Death's head,
Vapourer.

Ghost swift.

* Each word or phrase is the name of an actual moth.

Monorhyme

I am a woman, and dead
Where a woman lives, she said

I am the mirror I dread
With face to the wall, she said

I am the unruffled bed
And the buttoned blouse, she said

I am the hands and the head
And the hub of the house, she said

I loved, I bore, I bled,
I sit and knit, she said.

It's the Sea I Want

It's the sea I want,
Make no mistake,
Not the resorts
With boardinghouses
Pressed together and shivering,
Praying for sun
And central heating –
It's the sea I want,
The whole boiling,
Destructive, disruptive, sterilizing –
I think it's smashing

Undermining
This island,
Unpinning
Gorse and headland,
Arresting, without warrant,
Growth and sunlight.
Landscapes at risk,
Thumped with fists of wind,
Eaten up with a mouthful of mist,
Slump like a Stock Market
Suddenly into the Channel.
Down the long final slide
Go houses full of the dying,
Carefully tended gardens
Into the riot of salt . . .

While
All along
A population of cold
Shelled and speechless creatures

Waits, to inherit
The hot, hideous, restless
Chaos I've helped to make
In sixty industrious years.
Sixty industrious years
And the motorway from the Midlands
Have brought me down at last
To the level of the sea.
I see with the sea's eye.

It bites the cliffs,
Fondles the coast, and swings
Away again, out to sea,
Waving, waving,
Making no promises,
It spits back in our faces
The coins and cans of the beaches.

It's the sea I want,
Belting the land, breaking
All the rules, speaking
Its guttural, thrusting tongue.
It pays no taxes,
Cringes before no conscience
And carries its own prestige
On its naked, shining back.

It's the sea I want,
If it's not too late
To sit, and contemplate
The hard bright barbarous jewels
Of the totally indifferent sea:
Something I never made
And cannot be guilty of.

I have done with the pains of love.
Leave me alone with the sea,
That picks bones clean,
And was, and shall be.

From the Somerset Levels*

Little wet god,
Wood-one,
I was buried
Out there, in the sticks,
In the swamps,
Face-down, in the sodden causeway.
Floating in time, in peat,
I held
Everything up.

Within the entrails
Of the ancient trackway
In a man-made bird's-nest
Of criss-cross withies,
I God was lodged
To keep the traveller
On the proper path,
Orientated, upright,
Clear of engulfing muck.

Step on my face,
Step over me,
My back is broad enough,
My mouth
Drains away flood
From crop, cattle and hearth.
Pests
Know their master.

It was quiet here
In the soaking centuries.

Now
Courteously disinterred,
Throned behind glass,
I sit, withered,
Threatening to crack,
Watching drily
My new and noisy,
Attentive, thronging,
Highly perishable
Worshippers.

* A small wooden female image, roughly carved, was found during
the excavation of the prehistoric trackways.

Directions for Taking

Everyone should, all through life,
Hear the donkey bray
At the rising day,
Hurdy, gurdy, hurdy, gurdy,
Hear the donkey bray.

Everyone should, now and then,
See the peacock's tail
Spread a shivering sail,
Alleluia, alleluia,
See the peacock's tail.

Everyone should, sometime, sometime,
Feel the tiger's breath
Like a passing death,
Timor mortis, hoc est corpus,
Feel the tiger's breath.

Everyone should, ever, always,
Taste the human beast
Hot and manifest,
Amor, clamour, carnal carol,
Taste the human beast.

Everyone must, lastly, lastly
Smell the empty air,
Outside, everywhere,
And nobody, nobody, nobody, nobody,
No body standing there.

This Poem . . .

This poem is dangerous: it should not be left
Within the reach of children, or even of adults
Who might swallow it whole, with possibly
Undesirable side-effects. If you come across
An unattended, unidentified poem
In a public place, do not attempt to tackle it
Yourself. Send it (preferably, in a sealed container)
To the nearest centre of learning, where it will be rendered
Harmless, by experts. Even the simplest poem
May destroy your immunity to human emotions.
All poems must carry a Government warning. Words
Can seriously affect your heart.

People Etcetera

People are lovely to touch –
A nice warm sloppy tilting belly
Happy in its hollow of pelvis
Like a bowl of porridge.

People are fun to notice –
Their eyes taking off like birds
Away from their words
To settle on breasts and ankles
Irreverent as pigeons.

People are good to smell –
Leathery, heathery, culinary or Chanel,
Lamb's-wool, sea-salt, linen dried in the wind,
Skin fresh out of a shower.

People are delicious to taste –
Crisp and soft and tepid as new-made bread,
Tangy as blackberries, luscious as avocado,
Native as milk,
Acrid as truth.

People are irresistible to draw –
Hand following hand,
Eye outstaring eye,
Every curve an experience of self,
Felt weight of flesh, tension of muscle
And all the geology of an elderly face.

And people are easy to write about?
Don't say it.
What are these shadows
Vanishing
Round the
Corner?

The Death of Adam

I saw it coming,
The cold.
It must have been coming on a long time.
Ever since I'd known him.

Not surprising, really,
With him come up from the dust
And me from the bone.

Still, it was odd,
Watching it actually happen.
Everything sags; did you know?
I didn't know.

Teeth fall out, and then the face falls in.
Skin
Withers and wrinkles and shrivels like an apple
(Yes, like an apple)
And the top of the skull
(Where the hair and the brains keep complicated house
    together)
Becomes
Plain, smooth, simple,
Unoccupied by anything.

And he couldn't walk at all, nor talk at all
(We had to stop arguing about whose fault it was)
And the sun made his eyes hurt
And he had to leave the world that belonged to him
And the animals he'd given a name to
And the wife that was part of him,
To become a kind of collapse,
A remnant, something remembered,
Not all there any more.

He was always first at everything
And now
The first man ever to be dead.
Perhaps, as gardeners,
We should have learned from the leaves
What it means to be deciduous.

Will it always be just like this
For the rest of us?
Or must I look forward
To a separate, feminine, suitable
Method of disappearance?
Middle aged, but still naked
To man-stare and God-stare,
Covering myself up with my hands and my long grey hair,
Breasts falling like apples
And the small pool of darkness
Inside me
Gone dry?

The Watch-Dogs

Every day, the watch-dogs raise their muzzles
A little higher

They become more sensitive,
Reliable, subtle,
As the century ticks away

The watch-dogs
Do not bear looking at
Nor thinking of

They are very susceptible
To tremors and disaffection –
Do not upset them

They can hear grass growing
And the embryo quick in the womb

How long they will tolerate this
We do not know

The Passenger Opposite

British Rail

Everything falls asleep with sleep
    – The wariness, the will –
It's hard to loathe a sleeping face
Lapsed back into a state of grace,
     Naked, relaxed and still.

Even the hair is childish now,
     Rumpled and damp and young,
The teeth unclenched, the hands let loose,
Both smile and frown gone out of use,
     No message from the tongue.

The mouth has slackened, and the chin
     Given up its thrust and drive,
The eyes have left their sentry box,
The ears have closed their subtle locks.
     Content to be alive

Just breathing; and the eyelashes
     Are delicate, and long,
They stoop, and soothe the fretted cheek
Which knows no words nor need to speak,
     No scope for going wrong.

This is the sleep of train, and plane,
     Of hammock, bunk and pram,
Deck-chair and hospital and cot,
Of slaked desire, of world-forgot,
     Of I-Am-That-I-Am.

And if the shoulder's tapped, or shouts
   Disturb the rhythmic bliss,
Will the face resurrect its fears,
Its irritations and its years
   Or smile, and shape a kiss?

Here is my stop. I must get out
   And cannot answer this.

Water Aubrey

Places have to be invented
By those who discover them

On a hot afternoon, the street smelling of buses,
Silence congealing in the public library,
I found, among files and flies,
By casual alighting of the eyes,
Mention of Water Aubrey.

At once, imaginable rivers
Started, to water docile cattle.
The flies were tied by anglers. Trout sprang.
Among the bulky volumes of Natural History
Anonymous birds unseasonably sang.

I kept my eyes away from the gazetteer
And the map cupboard – sources of information
That might identify a railway junction,
Dismantled factories, a missile site,
Or mile after mile of nothing very much.

In a dusty rectangle of sunlight, wiping my spectacles,
Receiving and issuing books, nodding abstractedly
At hands, handbags, jacket-sleeves, tickets, apologies,
I walked in the cool shade of a couple of words,
Inventing Water Aubrey.

Country Life

Within half-a-mile, to my knowledge,
Two solitary alcoholics,
A divorce in progress,
Homes crumbling under nettles.

Badgers, nocturnally ambling,
The fox caught red-muzzled,
The owls hanging up night in inverted commas,
Molework.   The moon's partners.

Swamp waiting in patience
To suck down plough, or be ripped open.
Trees prevented from falling
Only by trees.   The furze-defended common.

Barbed-wire entanglement of stars. The river's
Gradual grovelling infiltration
Like a farm dog edging into the living-room.
And men.   And women.

from FURNISHED ROOMS

All the characters in Furnished Rooms *are imaginative — they live in bed-sitters in a haze of hope, fantasies, despair and routine; any resemblance to human beings is intentional. They have haunted me since my own bed-sitter days, and more persistently since I took part in the unavoidable closing-down of a boarding-house. The introductory poem, 'Notice', is not a satire on landlords, but sets out the regulations for living in a world created and controlled by Somebody Else.*

— Elma Mitchell

NOTICE

We will do our best to make your stay a pleasant one.
Please note the whereabouts of the Fire Exit.
We cannot contemplate children or animals.

Anything of value should be deposited
In safekeeping, and a receipt obtained.
Guests should not re-adjust the television.

Nothing to be prepared or consumed in the bedrooms.
Do not hang your personal laundry over the bath.
Put your ashes in the receptacles provided.

In case of illness, kindly contact the proprietor.
Please give adequate notice of your departure.
Make sure you leave nothing behind you when you go.

SCULPTRESS

Clay is reasonable
And quiet to work with.
No one could object to clay.
I wouldn't hold out for stone –
The weight, the dust, the blows,
The lovely devouring sounds –
I wouldn't insist on those.

I'm reasonable.

What harm can I do with clay?
Dirty stuff, they say,
Well, messy, anyway.
But I've taken down the curtains,
Rolled back the carpet, stripped the bed and hidden
The pictures somewhere – made a great improvement,
Even given unity to the wall-paper
(It's *red* clay I prefer)
And piled their other treasures outside the door
Out of work's way.

I squat on the floor
And men come out of my fingers
And beasts, and things
I wouldn't give a name to.

They have shadows, and move
Slowly around with the sun.
I am busy, watching them.

Is it Friday again? All right, I'm going to pay
Next week. No, don't come in.
You wouldn't like it. There are people here,
A tribe. They are listening.

Thank you. I am all right.

Another bill? From Harrods? My daughter will pay —
That bitch in the mink.
                    And, damn you, go away.

IT'S MOTHER, YOU SEE

It's mother, you see.

I cannot fold her up like a pram or a bicycle.
It's every day crawling around the agencies.
I cannot leave her alone in a furnished room.
She has to come with me, arm in arm, umbrella'd,
Or trailing a little.

She is thin in wind and limb,
She is not quite white in the head,
Now and then she stops — suddenly and completely
Like a mutinous dog on a lead.

(And once, long ago, in reverse,
I trailed after *her* skirts in the throng streets,
Her basket of goodies
Bobbing just out of my reach)

She's no need to stare at the shops.
We have plenty more clothes, if we bothered to open the cases,
And hundreds of photographs of the way things were.
Sometimes we take out a bit of the better china
And wash it and put it away again.

It is every day to the agents,
Then on to the library, checking the papers for ads.
Or walking the streets, looking for signs that might say
Where to apply for a key.

It is hard on the legs, it is hard on the wits and the heart,
But I cannot leave her alone in a furnished room.
O come *on*, Mum. One day we'll find us a home
Somewhere this side of the sky.

LETTER HOME

Dear Lucy,
Thought I would drop you a line, let you know I'm all right,
Seeing that you are in Bristol and I am in London,
Not far as the crow flies, but the time and the cash –
And I am no crow, as you know,
I have too many things to think of, to make a dash for it.

Dear Luce, I'm writing to say I would like to put
My arms round you and the children – but they aren't long
        enough!
Once a month, in Bristol, we meet, in the flesh, with luck.
You are much in my thoughts. Perhaps I am little in yours.

You know I could never write letters – and the telephone
Stands in the hall of my digs, with everyone listening
And expensive except for business. I can't ask my secretary
To write to my wife, although she remembers your birthday
And the children's; and we think about you on Fridays.

I like the smell of women, their hair and their skin
And their spiralling inwardness, and the way they can talk about
    nothing
At all hours, when it's cold. This is not the letter
I intended to write you, Lucy. So long, all my love.

Goodnight

SELF-PORTRAITS

The cupboard contains my dresses, the drawer my faces.
Seven selves lie on seven shelves.

I try them on every night, a concoction of fig-leaves
To cover all possible cases. I am Juliet,
Cleopatra, Marilyn – everyone, except naked
Susanna Smith, my mother and father's daughter.

I owe nobody the make of my body.
I bought myself at Boots – the cosmetic counter
And the slimming aids. I shopped for myself in windows
And women's magazines, and then in the long, long mirrors
In the eyes of the watchers of birds.

I twist my mouth in the glass. I peer anxiously,
And erase, and alter – the artist after perfection
With pencil and brush, the ladies' do-it-yourself
Portable Rembrandt, the only self-portrait that has to
Be painted afresh every morning.

Nice work, in its way –

Not boring, certainly, the supple capacity
To make oneself up as one goes, to carry the light
And rainbow style of continuous creation

But I like myself best in the bath, where it all comes off.

EXPATRIATE

Women are never in exile. There is always bread
Or milk to be got; the need to placate, to obtain,
To stopper the hungry mouth. Alone for a moment
In this featureless room rubbed by so many existences,
I begin to feather my nest – to nurture and warm
This orphan habitation, abandoned so often,
To see in its unloved surfaces, gritty corners,
Intimations of comfort and future familiarities –
To recognize already
In a wobbly doorknob or a speckled mirror
Those constant images that will accompany
Silence, Beethoven, the making of love.

ROOM MATES

They said, they couldn't take us both.
I said, they'd have to.

What *is* this – the Salvation Army?
They'll be praying over us next.

Our money's the same paper as anyone else's
And prompter.

We don't fiddle the meter or block the loo
We have other things to think of.

When freedom dawns (if it's not too wet a morning)
Someone may notice that it started here

And I don't mean with handgrenades
But inconspicuously and taken for granted.

LAST WORDS

Something is going to happen in this room
That needs no signature.

On the table, a bottle of whisky, a bottle of brandy,
A bottle of sleeping-pills. But that's not it.
Still life, perhaps; but not so still as that.

A room like this is a clutter of finger-prints
And furniture-polish: utterly empty of living.

It was near, a near thing – and gets yearly nearer.
I distinctly hear the procreant blackbird sing
In the shut suburban February garden.
I grasp realities in either hand.

Possibly righteousness and peace will kiss one another.
More probably not. Nothing can cheat us of silence.
The final condition of stillness needs no practice.

But now, at this point, as usual, taking two minutes
Of your valuable reading-time, depriving us both of
    solitude –

WORDS elbow their way into the room
Crashing the party
Without identification, without security,
Bearing no signature, wearing old clothes.

Some day I will have the last word.

ALL OUT

Miss Pilger left last
The Army took her away
Charitably.
A vacancy
There, in the head.

No need to advertise
To fill her place
Now it can stay
As empty as the rest.

Rest, rest!

At last I have the house as I would wish.
I've stripped their beds, and flayed
The floors of rugs
Nothing to gather dust, nothing to speak
Of messy flesh and blood.

The TV screen
Stands in the corner blank, in permanent punishment
For all those years of noisiness and fidgeting,
No cut and dying flowers injure the air
No underwear
Weeps in the bathroom, skulks in the airing cupboard.
The phone's been dislocated, strangled.
Meters and clocks have ceased to measure out
My time and energy
Since yesterday.

No typewriter taps, no needle knits, no kettle
Spits.
The echoes have gone, with the footsteps and the voices
And the complaints.
     The books are shut at last.
      The accounts are closed.

Clean sheets on a single bed
Wait, upstairs.
    I think I'll take myself off
Soon, pretty soon.

Charles Causley

Kelly Wood

Walking in Kelly Wood, gathering words
Frail as spilt leaves, fine sticks of sentences,
Spirals of bracken from the fallen ground,
I listen for the silences of stone,
The stream's white voice, the indifference of birds.
Safe in my quiet house I lay them out
– Leaf, stick and bracken – in the hearth's cold frame,
Strike steel on flint against the page of dark,
Wait patiently for the first spark. A flame.

Family Feeling

My Uncle Alfred had the terrible temper.
Wrapped himself up in its invisible cloak.
When the mood was on his children crept from the kitchen.
It might have been mined. Not even the budgie spoke.

He was killed in the First World War in Mesopotamia.
His widow rejoiced, though she never wished him dead.
After three years a postcard arrived from Southampton.
'Coming home Tuesday. Alf,' was what it said.

His favourite flower he called the antimirrhinum.
Grew it instead of greens on the garden plot.
Didn't care much for children, though father of seven.
Owned in his lifetime nine dogs all called Spot.

At Carnival time he rode the milkman's pony.
Son of the Sheikh, a rifle across his knee.
Alf the joiner as Peary in cotton-wool snowstorms.
Secret in cocoa and feathers, an Indian Cree.

I recognised him once as the Shah of Persia.
My Auntie's front-room curtains gave him away.
'It's Uncle Alf!' I said, but his glance was granite.
'Mind your own business, nosey,' I heard him say.

I never knew just what it was that bugged him,
Or what kind of love a father's love could be.
One by one the children baled out of the homestead.
'You were too young when yours died,' they explained to me.

Today, walking through St Cyprian's churchyard
I saw where he lay in a box the dry colour of bone.
The grass was tamed and trimmed as if for a Sunday.
Seven antimirrhinums in a jar of stone.

Bridie Wiles

Bridie Wiles, 2 Gas Court Lane,
Between the tanyard and the railway line,
About the time of the first Armistice
Scooped me, one Saturday, out of my pram.
Promised me the river.

My cousin Gwennie, nine,
And three foot eight to Bridie's five eleven
Said, 'You do
And I'll chuck you in too.
Anyway,
The water isn't deep enough today
To drown a frog in.'

'Nor is it,' Bridie said, sometimes
Quite sensible despite her role
As our local madwoman
Of Chaillot,
Making to bale me
Back into the pram,
If the wrong way round.

Decades on,
At Uncle Heber's Co-op funeral,
'I'll tell you something you don't know,'
Said Gwen.
'Between us, Bridie and me pulling
As if you were a Christmas cracker
We dropped you on your head.
I never told your mum. Or mine.
My God, but you went white!
We thought that you'd gone dead.

'Another thing.
It's always been a mystery to me
How you're the only one
Of our lot doing what you do.
The other day I read
That sort of thing can be set off
By a dint on the head.
Do you think that's true?
Perhaps you owe it all to Bridie and to me.'

I asked her what she meant by it and all.
'Not possible,' said cousin Gwen, 'to say.
Though Bridie may.'

Dick Lander

When we were children at the National School
We passed each day, clipped to the corner of
Old Sion Street, Dick Lander, six foot four,
Playing a game of trains with match-boxes.

He poked them with a silver-headed cane
In the seven kinds of daily weather God
Granted the Cornish. Wore a rusted suit.
It dangled off him like he was a tree.

My friend Sid Bull, six months my senior, and
A world authority on medicine,
Explained to me just what was wrong with Dick.
'Shell-shopped,' he said. 'You catch it in the war.'

We never went too close to Dick in case
It spread like measles. 'Shell-shopped, ain't you, Dick?'
The brass-voiced Sid would bawl. Dick never spoke.
Carried on shunting as if we weren't there.

My Auntie said before he went away
Dick was a master cricketer. Could run
As fast as light. Was the town joker. Had
Every girl after him. Was spoiled quite out

Of recognition, and at twenty-one
Looked set to take the family business on
(Builders' merchants, seed, wool, manure and corn).
'He's never done a day's work since they sent

'Him home after the Somme,' my Uncle grinned.
'If he's mazed as a brush, my name's Lord George.
Why worry if the money's coming in?'
At firework time we throw a few at Dick.

Shout, 'Here comes Kaiser Bill!' Dick stares us through
As if we're glass. We yell, 'What did you do
In the Great War?' And skid into the dark.
'Choo, choo,' says Dick. 'Choo, choo, choo, choo, choo, choo.'

First Day

For Moelwyn Merchant

Myope, jackdaw-tongued, I was fetched to school
Too early. ('Only child. Needs company.')
School was an ark of slate and granite, beached
Between the allotments and the castle ditch.

Cased on the roof, the famous Hanging Bell:
Came, 1840, from the county gaol.
I'm 1917, from Old Hill, rigged out
In regulation infant gear: knitted

Green jersey, cords snagging both knees, new boots
With tags that locked my feet together. Hold
The tin mug with my cocoa money in.
A washed September morning, and the gas

Was on. Over the teacher's desk I saw
A cross made out of wood. Small steps led up,
But nobody was on it. Miss Treglown
Was writing down my name in a big book.

'Where's Jesus?' Without lifting up her head,
'Jesus is everywhere,' Miss Treglown said.
As if on cue, trapped in its rusted tower,
The Hanging Bell came to. Banged out the hour.

My Enemy

My enemy was the pork butcher's son.
I see him, head and shoulders over me,
Sphinx-faced, his cheeks the colour of lard, the eyes
Revolver-blue through Bunter spectacles.
When we lined up for five to nine at school
He'd get behind me, crumple up a fist,
Stone thumb between the first and second fingers;
Punch out a tune across my harp of ribs.

Ten years ahead of Chamberlain, I tried
Appeasement, with the same results: gave him
My lunch of bread and cheese, the Friday bun,
The Lucky Bags we bought at Maggie Snell's.
One Armistice I wept through the Two Minutes
Because my dad was killed in France (not true).
'Poor little sod, his father's dead,' my enemy
Observed, discreetly thumping me again.

I took the scholarship exam not for
The promise of Latin, Greek, but to escape
My enemy. The pork butcher's sharp son
Passed too, and I remember how my heart
Fell like a bucket down a summer well
The day Boss Ward read out our names. And how,
Quite unaccountably, the torment stopped
Once we were at the Grammar. We've not met

Since 1939, although I heard
How as a gunner in the long retreat
Hauling the piece from Burma, he was met
At the first village by naked kids with stones,
Placards reading QUIT INDIA. After that,

Nothing; except our pair of sentences
To thirty years in chalk Siberias:
Which one of us is which hard to define
For children in the butcher's class, and mine.

Forbidden Games

A lifetime, and I see them still:
My aunt, my mother, silently
Held by the stove's unflinching eye
Inside the tall house scaled with slate.
The paper boy runs up the hill,
Cries, '*Echo!*' to the black-blown sky.
The tin clock on the kitchen shelf
Taps seven. And I am seven. And lie
Flat on the floor playing a game
Of Snakes & Ladders by myself.

Upstairs, my father in his bed,
Shadowed still by the German War,
A thin light burning at his head,
To me is no more than a name
That's also mine. I wonder what
The two women are waiting for.
My aunt puts down her library book.
My mother winds a bit of wool.
Each gives to each a blinded look.
'Your father's with the angels now.'
Which of them speaks I cannot tell.
And then I say to them, 'I know.'
And give the dice another throw.

From the poem sequence *Scenes of Childhood*

The Boot Man

'Thin as sliced bacon,' she would say, fingering
The soles. 'They're for the Boot Man.' And I'd go
Up Crab Lane, the slight wafer of words she doled
Me out with worrying my tongue. *Please, soled
And heeled by Saturday.*

                  She didn't know
That given speech, to me, refused to come.
I couldn't read aloud in class; sat dumb
In front of howling print; could never bring
On my bitched breath the words I should have said,
Though they were pummelling inside my head.

Somehow the Boot Man stanched my speeches more
Than all the rest. He'd watch me as I tried
To retch up words: his eyes a wash-tub blue,
Stork-head held sideways; braces threaded through
Loops in his long-johns. Once again my dead
Father stood there: army boots bright as glass,
Offering me a hand as colourless
As phosgene.

            And they told me time would cure
The irresolute tongue. But never said that I
Would meet again upon the faithless, sly
And every-morning page, the Boot Man's eye.

Recruiting Drive

Under the willow the willow
  I heard the butcher-bird sing,
Come out you fine young fellow
  From under your mother's wing.
I'll show you the magic garden
  That hangs in the beamy air,
The way of the lynx and the angry Sphinx
  And the fun of the freezing fair.

Lie down lie down with my daughter
  Beneath the Arabian tree,
Gaze on your face in the water
  Forget the scribbling sea.
Your pillow the nine bright shiners
  Your bed the spilling sand,
But the terrible toy of my lily-white boy
  Is the gun in his innocent hand.

You must take off your clothes for the doctor
  And stand as straight as a pin,
His hand of stone on your white breastbone
  Where the bullets all go in.
They'll dress you in lawn and linen
  And fill you with Plymouth gin,
O the devil may wear a rose in his hair
  I'll wear my fine doe-skin.

My mother weeps as I leave her
  But I tell her it won't be long,
The murderers wail in Wandsworth Gaol
  But I shoot a more popular song.

Down in the enemy country
  Under the enemy tree
There lies a lad whose heart has gone bad
  Waiting for me, for me.

He says I have no culture
  And that when I've stormed the pass
I shall fall on the farm with a smoking arm
  And ravish his bonny lass.
Under the willow the willow
  Death spreads her dripping wings
And caught in the snare of the bleeding air
  The butcher-bird sings, sings, sings.

Chief Petty Officer

He is older than the naval side of British history,
And sits
More permanent than the spider in the enormous wall.
His barefoot, coal-burning soul
Expands, puffs like a toad, in the convict air
Of the Royal Naval Barracks at Devonport.

Here, in depot, is his stone Nirvana:
More real than the opium pipes,
The uninteresting relics of his Edwardian foreign commission.
And, from his thick stone box,
He surveys with a prehistoric eye the hostilities-only ratings.

He has the face of the dinosaur
That sometimes stares from old Victorian naval photographs:
That of some elderly lieutenant
With boots and a celluloid Crippen collar,
Brass buttons and cruel ambitious eyes of almond.

He was probably made a Freemason in Hong Kong.
He has a son (on War Work) in the Dockyard,
And an appalling daughter
In the WRNS.
He writes on your draft-chit,
Tobacco permit or request-form
In a huge antique Borstal hand,
And pins notices on the board in the Chiefs' Mess
Requesting his messmates not to
Lay on the billiard table.
He is an anti-Semite, and has somewhat reactionary views,
And reads the pictures in the daily news.

And when you return from the nervous Pacific
Where the seas
Shift like sheets of plate-glass in the dazzling morning;
Or when you return
Browner than Alexander, from Malta,
Where you have leaned over the side, in harbour,
And seen in the clear water
The salmon-tins, wrecks and tiny explosions of crystal fish,
A whole war later
He will still be sitting under a pusser's* clock
Waiting for tot-time,
His narrow forehead ruffled by the Jutland wind.

pusser's: strictly naval; naval issue.

Richard Bartlett

Reading the ninety-year-old paper singed
By time, I meet my shadowed grandfather,
Richard Bartlett, stone-cutter, quarryman;
The Bible Christian local preacher, Sunday
School teacher and teetotaller. *Highly*
Respected, leading and intelligent
Member of the sect. He will be greatly missed.
Leaves wife and family of seven children,
The youngest being three months old.

Nine on a July morning: Richard Bartlett
About to split a stone, trying to find
A place to insert the wedge. The overhang
Shrugs off a quiet sting of slate. It nags
Three inches through the skull. Richard Bartlett
Never spoke after he was struck. Instead
Of words the blood and brains kept coming.
They lugged him in a cart to the Dispensary.
Never a chance of life, the doctors said.
He lived until twelve noon. His mate, Melhuish,
Searched for, but never found, the killing stone.
The fees of the jury were given to the widow.

The funeral was a thunder of hymns and prayers.
Two ministers, churchyard a checkerboard
Pieced with huge black: the family nudged nearer
The pit where the Workhouse was, and a leper's life
On the Parish. And in my grandmother
Was lit a sober dip of fear, unresting
Till her death in the year of the Revolution:
Her children safely fled like beads of mercury
Over the scattered map. I close the paper,

Its print of mild milk-chocolate. Bend to the poem,
Trying to find a place to insert the wedge.

Uncle Stan

Here's Uncle Stan, his hair a comber, slick
In his Sundays, buttoning a laugh;
Gazing, sweet-chestnut eyed, out of a thick
Ship's biscuit of a studio photograph.
He's Uncle Stan, the darling of our clan,
Throttled by celluloid: the slow-worm thin
Tie, the dandy's rose, Kirk Douglas chin
Hatched on the card in various shades of tan.

He died when I was in my pram; became
The hero of my child's mythology.
Youngest of seven, gave six of us his name
If not his looks, and gradually he
Was Ulysses, Jack Marvel, Amyas Leigh.
Before the Kaiser's war, crossed the grave sea
And to my mother wrote home forest tales
In Church School script of bears and waterfalls.

I heard, a hundred times, of how and when
The blacksmith came and nipped off every curl
('So that he don't look too much like a girl')
And how Stan tried to stick them on again.
As quavering children, how they dragged to feed
The thudding pig; balanced on the sty-beams,
Hurled bucket, peelings on its pitching head –
Fled, twice a day, from its enormous screams.

I watched the tears jerk on my mother's cheek
For his birth day; and gently she would speak
Of how time never told the way to quell
The brisk pain of their whistle-stop farewell:

A London train paused in the winter-bleak
Of Teignmouth. To his older friend said, 'Take
Good care of him.' Sensed, from a hedging eye,
All that was said when neither made reply.

I look at the last photograph. He stands
In wrinkled khaki, firm as Hercules,
Pillars of legs apart, and in his hands
A cane; defying the cold lens to ease
Forward an inch. Here's Uncle Stan, still game,
As Private, 1st Canadians, trimmed for war.
Died at Prince Rupert, B.C. And whose name
Lives on, in confident brass, for evermore.

That's all I know of Uncle Stan. Those who
Could tell the rest are flakes of ash, lie deep
As Cornish tin, or flatfish. 'Sweet as dew,'
They said. Yet – what else made them keep
His memory fresh as a young tree? Perhaps
The lure of eyes, quick with large love, is clue
To what I'll never know, and the bruised maps
Of other hearts will never lead me to.
He might have been a farmer; swallowed mud
At Vimy, Cambrai; smiling, have rehearsed
To us the silent history of his blood:
But a Canadian winter got him first.

Photograph

She walks among time-beaten stones
One hand upon the rood beam stair
That rises out of sticks and grass
Into a nothingness of air.

Here, where the abbey's great ship struck
And bramble bushes curve and sprout
She stands her granite-sprinkled ground
And stares the speering camera out.

She's dressed for Sunday: finest serge,
The high-necked blouse, a golden pin.
My grandmother: who sewed and scrubbed,
Cleaned out the church, took washing in.

Too soon, my mother said, too soon
The hands were white and washed to bone;
The seven children grown and gone,
And suddenly a life was done.

Today I stand where she once stood
And stranded arch and column sprawl,
Watching where still the ivy streams
In torrents down the abbey wall.

And still the many-noted rooks
About the tree-tops rail and run;
Still, at my feet, the celandine
Opens its gold star to the sun.

Firm as a figurehead she stands,
Sees with unsparing eye the thread
Of broken words within my hand
And will not turn away her head.

I Love the Laurel Green

After Etienne Jodelle

I love the laurel green, whose verdant flame
Burns its bright victory on the winter day,
Calls to eternity its happy nàme
And neither time nor death shall wear away.

I love the holly tree with branches keen,
Each leaflet fringed with daggers sharp and small.
I love the ivy, too, winding its green,
Its ardent stem about the oak, the wall.

I love these three, whose living green and true
Is as unfailing as my love for you
Always by night and day whom I adore.

Yet the green wound that stays within me more
Is ever greener than these three shall be:
Laurel and ivy and the holly tree.

Ballad of the Bread Man

Mary stood in the kitchen
   Baking a loaf of bread.
An angel flew in through the window.
   'We've a job for you,' he said.

'God in his big gold heaven,
   Sitting in his big blue chair,
Wanted a mother for his little son.
   Suddenly saw you there.'

Mary shook and trembled,
   'It isn't true what you say.'
'Don't say that,' said the angel.
   'The baby's on its way.'

Joseph was in the workshop
   Planing a piece of wood.
'The old man's past it,' the neighbours said.
   'That girl's been up to no good.'

'And who was that elegant fellow,'
   They said, 'in the shiny gear?'
The things they said about Gabriel
   Were hardly fit to hear.

Mary never answered,
   Mary never replied.
She kept the information,
   Like the baby, safe inside.

It was election winter.
   They went to vote in town.
When Mary found her time had come
   The hotels let her down.

The baby was born in an annexe
  Next to the local pub.
At midnight, a delegation
  Turned up from the Farmers' Club.

They talked about an explosion
  That made a hole in the sky,
Said they'd been sent to the Lamb & Flag
  To see God come down from on high.

A few days later a bishop
  And a five-star general were seen
With the head of an African country
  In a bullet-proof limousine.

'We've come,' they said, 'with tokens
  For the little boy to choose.'
Told the tale about war and peace
  In the television news.

After them came the soldiers
  With rifle and bomb and gun,
Looking for enemies of the state.
  The family had packed and gone.

When they got back to the village
  The neighbours said, to a man,
'That boy will never be one of us,
  Though he does what he blessed well can.'

He went round to all the people
  A paper crown on his head.
Here is some bread from my father.
  Take, eat, he said.

Nobody seemed very hungry.
  Nobody seemed to care.
Nobody saw the god in himself
  Quietly standing there.

He finished up in the papers.
    He came to a very bad end.
He was charged with bringing the living to life.
    No man was that prisoner's friend.

There's only one kind of punishment
    To fit that kind of a crime.
They rigged a trial and shot him dead.
    They were only just in time.

They lifted the young man by the leg,
    They lifted him by the arm,
They locked him in a cathedral
    In case he came to harm.

They stored him safe as water
    Under seven rocks.
One Sunday morning he burst out
    Like a jack-in-the-box.

Through the town he went walking.
    He showed them the holes in his head.
Now do you want any loaves? he cried.
    'Not today,' they said.

At the British War Cemetery, Bayeux

I walked where in their talking graves
And shirts of earth five thousand lay,
When history with ten feasts of fire
Had eaten the red air away.

'I am Christ's boy,' I cried. 'I bear
In iron hands the bread, the fishes.
I hang with honey and with rose
This tidy wreck of all your wishes.

'On your geometry of sleep
The chestnut and the fir-tree fly,
And lavender and marguerite
Forge with their flowers an English sky.

'Turn now towards the belling town
Your jigsaws of impossible bone,
And rising read your rank of snow
Accurate as death upon the stone.'

About your easy heads my prayers
I said with syllables of clay.
'What gift,' I asked, 'shall I bring now
Before I weep and walk away?'

Take, they replied, *the oak and laurel.*
Take our fortune of tears and live
Like a spendthrift lover. All we ask
Is the one gift you cannot give.

I am the Great Sun

From a Normandy crucifix of 1632

I am the great sun, but you do not see me,
  I am your husband, but you turn away.
I am the captive, but you do not free me,
  I am the captain you will not obey.

I am the truth, but you will not believe me,
  I am the city where you will not stay,
I am your wife, your child, but you will leave me,
  I am that God to whom you will not pray.

I am your counsel, but you do not hear me,
  I am the lover whom you will betray,
I am the victor, but you do not cheer me,
  I am the holy dove whom you will slay.

I am your life, but if you will not name me,
Seal up your soul with tears, and never blame me.

Night before a Journey

Books on the printed wall
Withhold their speech;
Pencil and paper and pen
Move out of reach.

The longcase clock in the hall
Winds carefully down.
No matter, says the house-ghost.
He is already gone.

A flower fallen on the shelf,
The stain of moon, of sun,
A wine-glass forgotten –
All await the return.

Nothing in the stopped house
Shall unbalance the air.
There is one, says the house-ghost,
Who is always here,

Patiently watching, waiting,
Moving from room to stilled room,
Light as breath, clear as light.
This, too, is his home.

When shall we meet, the stranger
And I, one with another?
When you leave for the last time,
Says the house-ghost. And together.

Flying

Flying over the crumpled hide of Spain,
Seville to Barcelona, the pinned-out skin
Curing in dusty light, I watch a thin
Skein after endless skein of road, mule-track
Thread the wild secrecy of valleys, lap
Impossible hills, and on the sudden plain
Meet other paths; as swiftly part again.

The Moorish castle spoils above the town.
Houses, spilt sugar-lumps, coagulate
Around a church half-eaten by sun. A neat
Gethsemane of olives, grey as slate,
Spreads like a shadow. Stubs of rock stitch lean
Watercourses, sand-beds, in slanting heat.
The land aches with the first green thrust of wheat.

So much to blunt the eye! And still I hear
The squealing bands behind the *pasos*: stare
At porters shouldering wounded Jesus down
Holy Week; the unblemished penitents,
Masked, in fools' caps; the Holy Virgin fenced
By thickets of candle-flame, her shaken crown
A foliage of stars, her wax tears spent.

The ladder-man adjusts the soldier's lance,
Re-lights dead candles, fixes Pilate's cloak.
Crowds flood the *avenida* like a dam.
I squat by the cathedral on a rung
Of broken stone. And suddenly the young
Gypsy from the Trianas, peddling Coke,
Smiles frankly, makes to pass me by, but first
Runs through me with brilliant, uncasual glance.

Sees me for what I was, for what I am.
Offers a cup. Having observed my thirst.

Grandmother

Rises before the first bird. Slugs about
In gig-sized slippers. Soothes the anxious whine
Of the washing-machine with small bequests
Collected from our room. Whacks up the blind.
Restores a lost blanket. Firmly ignores,
With total grace, your nakedness. And mine.

At seven the kitchen's a lit quarter-deck.
She guillotines salami with a hand
Veined like Silesia. Deals black, damp bread,
Ingots of butter, cheese, eggs grenade-strong.
Thinks, loudly, in ground German. Sends a long
And morning glance across anonymous crops
To where the *autobahn*, fluent with cars,
Spools north to Frankfurt, and unpromised land.

The clock, carted from Prague, hazards an hour.
A neighbour's child appears, failed priest at eight
In shirt and table-runner; ruptures mass
From *Hänsel und Gretel*. Does his holy best
To trip her. Filches sugar, sausage. Spoils
Her apron-strings. She lets it all go by
With the same shrug she gave when the burst car
Refused to let us vamp it into life,
And her to church. Perhaps it was the same
In Hitler's thirties: the Sudeten farm
Left in a moment, and her history
Carried in paper bags beneath each arm.

Her face is like a man's: a Roman beak
Caesar might quail at; and the squat, square frame
An icon of compassion. As she turns

Towards the leaning light, behind her eye
Burn embers of Europe's foul allegory.
Her body bears its harsh stigmata, dug
With easy instruments of blood and bone.
And still, I'm certain, she could up and stick
A yelling pig, a priest, a partisan
With equal mercy. Or a lack of it.
She's wise as standing-stones. Her gift of years
Almost persuades belief in God, the Devil;
Their parallel unease. Both heaven and hell
Entirely unprepared for her arrival.

Friedrich

Friedrich, at twenty-two,
Sumptuously bankrupt,
Bought a garage:
Every fuel-tank ailing.

Also a mobilisation
Of motor-bikes. Owes
A butcher's ransom
Of Deutschmarks. Has bikes

In the bathroom, kitchen,
Closets, bedroom.
To use the landing lavatory you have
To aim between two Suzukis.

He's a graceful mover; slim as
A fern-tree. Has a dancer's
Small bottom. His wife Peachy's
A sorceress. They don't

Say much when I'm around
But I know they've something
Going between them better than
Collected Poems, a T.S.B. account,

Twelve lines in *Gems
Of Modern Quotations*
And two (not war) medals.
Today, Friedrich

Sat for three hours
Earthed by the ears
To a Sony Sound System.
I couldn't hear

The music, only
Him singing. It was like
A speared hog. *Love*,
Skirled Friedrich, *'s when a cloud*

Fades in the blue
'N there's me, 'n there's you.
'N it's true.
Peachy brings in Coke

And Black Forest *gâteau*.
Their mutual gaze
Broaches each other's eye.

Next week he'll be Vasco da Gama.

At the Church of St Anthony, Lisbon

Plump as a Christmas chicken, Fra Antonio
Throbs in the north aisle at a beach of candles;
Clutches, as hand luggage, a conker-coloured
Bible; three little sparking lilies. Handles
His uprising cooler than airline captains: dealing
One foot towards the faithful, a long gaze
Past the chipped saints and the once-painted ceiling
Up to the time-burnt dome, flayed pink and blue,
The burst glass, and the sharp light squinting through.

Tricked by an autumn change of clock, we come
To Mass an hour too soon. A sacristan
On saint-duty points, wordless, to the birth-
Place, marbled wall to wall, and scrubbed
Vanilla-white. It's like a hospital
For sin. Smells wickedly of wax. We scan
Pencilled memorials, prayers, winking stones.
The reliquary's heart of yellow bone
Bays like a brass-section. No sense of loss
That the saint's tongue is in another place.

Blessèd St Anthony, the silver speaker,
Patron of firemen, preacher to Muslims, fishes:
Who asked for, and received, nothing: for whom
The wild ass knelt before the Host as witness
To Christ within the Eucharist: eldest son
Of chaste St Francis, who woke in a vision,
The Child Jesus in his bright arms – the heart
Shies at the thought of your incarnate tongue,
Its taste of iron, of flowers, on my own;
My disbelief, its quiet comfort, gone.

In Padua the day you died, the children
Ran the white streets. Cried, 'Anthony is dead!
Our father Anthony!' And at your sainting
Bells rang, unbidden. On this Lisbon morning,
The Tagus furling into the quick bay,
A donkey, ballasted with guttering, passes.
Neither the time nor place for miracles!
It stops, but not to kneel, before the Host
Of huge stone over me. No magical
Message from Padua; the unpulled bells
Silently lurching high above my head.
St Anthony, our father, is not dead.

Ten Types of Hospital Visitor

I

The first enters wearing the neon armour
Of virtue.
Ceaselessly firing all-purpose smiles
At everyone present
She destroys hope
In the breasts of the sick,
Who realise instantly
That they are incapable of surmounting
Her ferocious goodwill.

Such courage she displays
In the face of human disaster!

Fortunately, she does not stay long.
After a speedy trip round the ward
In the manner of a nineteen-thirties destroyer
Showing the flag in the Mediterranean,
She returns home for a week
– With luck, longer –
Scorched by the heat of her own worthiness.

II

The second appears, a melancholy splurge
Of theological colours;
Taps heavily about like a healthy vulture
Distributing deep-frozen hope.

The patients gaze at him cautiously.
Most of them, as yet uncertain of the realities
Of heaven, hell-fire, or eternal emptiness,

Play for safety
By accepting his attentions
With just-concealed apathy,
Except one old man, who cries
With newly sharpened hatred,
'Shove off! Shove off!
'Shove . . . shove . . . shove . . . shove
Off!
Just you
Shove!'

III

The third skilfully deflates his weakly smiling victim
By telling him
How the lobelias are doing,
How many kittens the cat had,
How the slate came off the scullery roof,
And how no one has visited the patient for a fortnight
Because everybody
Had colds and feared to bring the jumpy germ
Into hospital.

The patient's eyes
Ice over. He is uninterested
In lobelias, the cat, the slate, the germ.
Flat on his back, drip-fed, his face
The shade of a newly dug-up Pharaoh,
Wearing his skeleton outside his skin,
Yet his wits as bright as a lighted candle,
He is concerned only with the here, the now,
And requires to speak
Of nothing but his present predicament.

It is not permitted.

IV

The fourth attempts to cheer
His aged mother with light jokes
Menacing as shell-splinters.
'They'll soon have you jumping round
Like a gazelle,' he says.
'Playing in the football team.'
Quite undeterred by the sight of kilos
Of plaster, chains, lifting-gear,
A pair of lethally designed crutches,
'You'll be leap-frogging soon,' he says.
'Swimming ten lengths of the baths.'

At these unlikely prophecies
The old lady stares fearfully
At her sick, sick offspring
Thinking he has lost his reason –

Which, alas, seems to be the case.

V

The fifth, a giant from the fields
With suit smelling of milk and hay,
Shifts uneasily from one bullock foot
To the other, as though to avoid
Settling permanently in the antiseptic landscape.
Occasionally he looses a scared glance
Sideways, as though fearful of what intimacy
He may blunder on, or that the walls
Might suddenly close in on him.

He carries flowers, held lightly in fingers
The size and shape of plantains,

Eden Rock

They are waiting for me somewhere beyond Eden Rock:
My father, twenty-five, in the same suit
Of Genuine Irish Tweed, his terrier Jack
Still two years old and trembling at his feet.

My mother, twenty-three, in a sprigged dress
Drawn at the waist, ribbon in her straw hat,
Has spread the stiff white cloth over the grass.
Her hair, the colour of wheat, takes on the light.

She pours tea from a Thermos, the milk straight
From an old HP sauce bottle, a screw
Of paper for a cork; slowly sets out
The same three plates, the tin cups painted blue.

The sky whitens as if lit by three suns.
My mother shades her eyes and looks my way
Over the drifted stream. My father spins
A stone along the water. Leisurely,

They beckon to me from the other bank.
I hear them call, 'See where the stream-path is!
Crossing is not as hard as you might think.'

I had not thought that it would be like this.

Acknowledgements

The poems in this selection are taken from the following books, to whose publishers acknowledgement is made: *Side Effects* (Peterloo Poets, 1978), *Standing To* (Peterloo Poets, 1982), *Voices Off* (Peterloo Poets, 1984), *A Watching Brief* (Peterloo Poets, 1987), *Neck-Verse* (Peterloo Poets, 1992) and *Safe as Houses* (Peterloo Poets, 1995) for U.A. Fanthorpe; *The Poor Man in the Flesh* (Peterloo Poets, 1976), *The Human Cage* (Peterloo Poets, 1979), *Furnished Rooms* (Peterloo Poets, 1983) and *People Etcetera: Poems New and Selected* (Peterloo Poets, 1987) for Elma Mitchell; *Union Street* (Rupert Hart-Davis, 1957), *Underneath the Water* (Macmillan, 1968), *Collected Poems* (Macmillan, 1975), *Secret Destinations* (Macmillan, 1984), *Jack the Treacle Eater* (Macmillan Children's Books, 1987), *A Field of Vision* (Macmillan, 1988) and *Collected Poems* (new edition, Macmillan, 1992) for Charles Causley.